BASS WISDOM

BASS WISDOM

HOMER CIRCLE

ILLUSTRATIONS BY ROD WALINCHUS

THE LYONS PRESS
Guilford, Connecticut
An imprint of The Globe Pequot Press

To my "Childbride" of sixty years, Gayle, whom I courted for five years, until we could afford to marry. By that time she knew what it would mean to be hitched to a bass-bitten husband, but she persevered to become my best fishing buddy and toughest competition.

Also to my teammates at *Sports Afield* for thirty-two years of association as an editor with some of the outdoor world's most dedicated fellow editors and comrades. With special thanks to Ted Kesting whose faith in my writing ability opened the door to my career as an outdoor journalist.

I know of no man more blessed!

Uncle Homer and his Childbride. Photograph by Glen Lau.

Contents

Introduction

My obsession with bass began at the impressionable age of twelve, when a neighborhood buddy and his dad, both also named Homer, took me along to fish southern Ohio streams. Had bass been easy to catch, I doubt I'd be writing this book, but the ongoing challenge of not getting skunked addicted me.

During my junior year of high school, my civics teacher was a farmer with a two-acre pond that had some bass. With his blessing I planted in his pond about a dozen bass in the 5- to 7-pound range, taken from waters about an hour's drive away. One 6-pounder so fascinated me that I fished for her almost every afternoon after school, and she taught me a great deal about the senses of bass.

Her territory was by a sawed-off stump, and the one lure she preferred above all others was a Shakespeare mouse. Usually she'd blast it the first or second cast. After several months of catch and release, her mouth was puckered with scar tissue, but I never caught her twice the same day.

This taught me that bass have a memory, but a short one. It also taught me that hunger wasn't her only motive for grabbing that mouse, because many times her stomach was bloated with food. She was being territorial, attacking intruders into her domain.

Every time I learned something about bass behavior my fascination grew. I spent my weekends fishing area lakes and streams, and I began reading anything I could find on bass. The thought never entered my young mind that one day I'd be writing a book on the subject.

But here it is, more than a half century of catchings, skunkings, studying, writing, teaching, and pursuing this wondrous and enigmatic critter. Join me in my journalistic bass boat while I share my acquired lore with you.

1 The Basses

Ichthyologists recognize six species of bass and four subspecies. But only three species have a sufficiently broad distribution to be of general interest. These are the largemouth bass *(Micropterus salmoides)*, smallmouth bass *(Micropterus dolomieui)*, and the spotted bass *(Micropterus punctulatus)*. Each has its own solid following and a list of colloquial names as long as your favorite bass rod.

For instance, the largemouth bass is variously called bass, bigmouth, black bass, green bass, linesides, mossback, lake bass, Welshman, and anviljaw. Smallmouth are called bass, green bass, brownie, bronzeback, redeye, green trout, tiger bass, and smallie. Spotted bass are called linesides, green bass, green trout, diamond bass, Kentucky bass, southern bass, and rocky bass. The challenge comes in distinguishing one from another. Here's how:

- **Largemouth bass:** Look at the jaw joint, or *maxillary*, if you want to be technical. The flap, or extreme tip, ends *well behind the rear arc of the eye*. Next, check the dorsal fin, which has a spiny segment in front and a soft segment behind. These are divided in the middle where they join the back. Body markings vary so much they aren't dependable for identification.

- **Smallmouth bass:** Again, look at the jaw joint. It ends *below the middle of the eye*. The spiny and soft dorsals are high on both ends

largemouth bass

smallmouth bass

spotted bass

and low in the middle, but they are *continuous,* not divided as with the largemouth.

- **Spotted bass:** The jaw joint ends *below the rear arc of the eye* and the dorsals are continuous as on the smallmouth. However, the spotted bass has one (nearly) unique feature: Run your fingertip over its tongue; in the approximate center you'll feel a rough patch. These are rudimentary teeth, found in 98 percent of all spotted bass. Unfortunately, about 2 percent of largemouth and smallmouth bass also have this patch of teeth. Still, it's a pretty reliable spotted-bass identifier.

Of course, none of these three greats is a true bass at all. They're not even related to bass. Taxonomically, they belong to the sunfish family, *Centrarchidae,* which includes the rock bass, bluegill, crappie, and some twenty-two other species. The true basses belong to the family *Seranidae,* which includes the striped bass, white bass, yellow bass, and, by gosh, the yellow and white perches. Which makes the entire bass question a confused kettle of fish, except for one thing: Bassin' guys and gals don't give a hoot what taxonomists call largemouth, smallmouth, and spotted basses. Look how they screwed up the perches! To bass anglers, all these great fish are bass.

BIOLOGICAL FACTS

One of the main reasons our three basses are classified as sunfishes is their method of spawning. The male sets up housekeeping by fanning a nest until his tail is worn down. Then he selects a female, woos her onto the nest, and in a brief moment of ecstasy (although you can't tell by the expression on that pug-ugly face), it's over.

The female helps guard the eggs for a day, then she departs, leaving ol' dad to rear the bass kids and defend them valiantly against the relentless gangs of raiding bluegills. One or two rush at him, he chases them, and other bluegills dash in to grab mouthfuls of eggs before the defender can return to scatter them. Add to egg predation a drastic mortality from fungus, bacteria, and many water-world predators, and the bass has an extremely hazardous existence. On average, about one bass in 6,000 survives to maturity. Knowing this, I handle every bass I catch with gentle care. This is a special creature I have been privileged to catch and release.

WORLD RECORDS

If you have a yen to make bass history as a world-record champion in any of these species, here are the weights you'll need to top:

- Largemouth bass, 22¼ pounds, caught in 1932 by George Perry in Montgomery Lake, Georgia

- Smallmouth bass, 11 pounds, 15 ounces, caught in 1955 by David Hayes in Dale Hollow Lake, Kentucky

- Spotted bass, 8 pounds, 10½ ounces, caught in 1972 by Billy Henderson in Smith Lake, Alabama

No one doubts that bigger bass are out there waiting for a lucky angler to present the right lure in its lair, but where will the next world records come from? The next record smallmouth could well live in the better-kept waters of Tennessee, Kentucky, Alabama, Arkansas, Georgia, and, coming on strong, California or Texas. These same waters may hold the next record spotted bass as well.

As for the next world-record largemouth, it simmers down to Florida, Texas, or California, with the latter most likely to come through. Two dying bass weighing more than the present record have been picked up there, and older bass are sure to be in the same waters.

Despite the lofty claims coming from Mexico and the Cuban lakes now being reopened, the chances of a record bass existing there are nil. Here's why: As manager of *Sports Afield*'s Fishing Awards Program for the past twenty-five years, I kept a ten-year record of all bass more than 10 pounds, putting a dot on a map where each entry was caught. Only three came from south of the frost line that runs through northern Florida's Marion County. Why should this be?

The clue comes from examining a scale from a bass south of this line: It has no annular rings, like the rings of a tree. Only bass caught north of this line have annular rings, which indicate a "slowing down" period in winter when their metabolism is lower. Afterward they gorge and grow fast, maturing in little more than a year. South of this line, however, the absence of annular rings indicates that bass have no winter hiatus. They grow faster but they die younger—before they can reach record size.

It's no coincidence that Uncle Homer and his childbride of sixty years live in Marion County, Florida!

One final observation on the three basses. I've caught them over much of their domain and I admire all three for their sporting qualities. I like the largemouth for its giant size, jolting strikes, brutish strength, skyward leaps, enduring battles, and bountiful memories. The same can be said of the high-spirited smallmouth, a native of crisper climes and covers—firmer in feel than the largemouth and faster in its continuous and frantic dashes for freedom. It's an Olympian.

But there's something a tad more special about the spotted bass. There's never a doubt about a pickup when this species jolts a lure. In many ways it's like the smallmouth, but I give it the edge not only in impact but also in endurance and determination to escape. Whether in a livewell or on a stringer, a spotted bass will explode all day long in frantic attempts to get free.

It's not easy to play favorites; all three species combine to make the bass America's favorite sport fish, and each has played an important role in my fishing/writing career. But if I found myself on a lake where all three were available, I believe I'd begin each day seeking that spotted character!

2 The World of the Bass

Where bass live

As with all wild creatures, cover is the word. A bass seeks cover for two reasons: ambush and sanctuary. When hungry, a bass lies in heavy cover where it can rush out to grab passing prey. After gorging, it seeks deep, heavy cover to digest and rest.

Bass hang out around weeds, lily pads, logs, brush, debris, fallen timber, docks, pilings, dark pockets, rocks, undercut banks, shore indentations, wrecks, reefs, shoals, and any midlake structure differing from surrounding bottom contours.

The big question is, which of these covers will bass be in when you hit the water? Ah, that's the challenge of bass catching, and we'll cover that in detail in later chapters.

What bass eat

Virtually anything digestible that moves or hides in the bass's domain, such as minnows and fry of all species, frogs, snakes, crawfish, freshwater shrimp, worms, insects, eels, snails, leeches, and small birds.

How bass eat

When you see a bass take a bait, it appears to grab it and gulp it down, all in a flash. Let me slow this down so you'll know the mechanics and be a better bass catcher. As a bass approaches its prey, it suddenly opens its jaws while simultaneously flaring its gills, creating an amazingly

A large female bass is combing bottom cover for prey. Note how the coloration camouflages her against the rippled background. Most large bass are loners and very protective of their lairs, chasing off intruders—including artificial lures.

strong suction that propels the object into the bass's cavernous mouth. This can be a strong take that the angler feels at once or a gentle take only an expert can detect.

This means that you must keep your mind attuned to the lure at the end of your line and your eyes locked onto the line where it enters the water. The instant you detect the slightest change, either in feel or in line attitude, set the hook *now*; a second later can be too late!

Why bass strike artificial lures

It's much too simplistic to say that a bass takes a lure because it's hungry and the lure looks edible. Experiences and experiments have proven that bass are motivated by far more than this. Here are eight reasons why I believe bass hit artificial lures: hunger, greed, gluttony, protective instinct, curiosity, reflexive action, anger, and territorial aggression. Some ten years ago I listed these in a *Sports Afield* article, and other writers have since adopted them. That's life. Here's why I believe as I do.

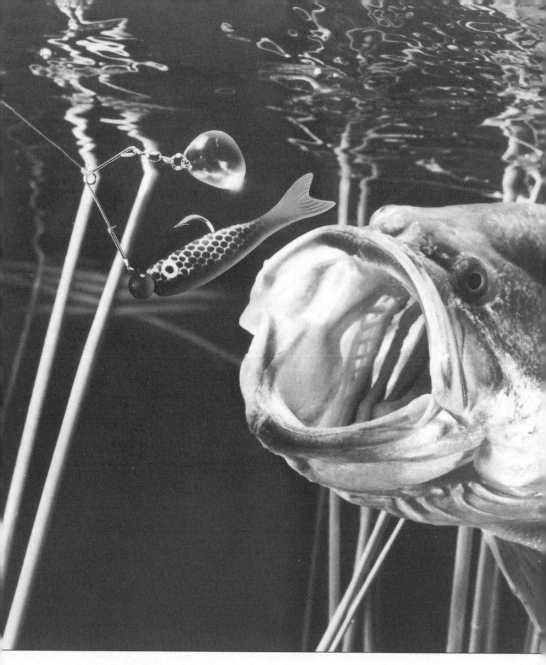

This closeup of a bass about to inhale an overhead spinnerbait sparks salient questions. One popular theory as to why bass take a spinnerbait is that bass think the body is a minnow after something to eat—the spinner. But this underwater shot shows a spinner behind the minnow, which blows this theory. Another theory is that in order to take a lure, a bass must open its mouth and flare its gills to create a flow of intake water, which sucks in the lure. What better proof than the sight of that wide-open mouth and those flared gills! I believe!

Year-class bass are ganging up in search of food. At times younger bass act as "flushers," crashing into minnow schools, while older bass follow for easy pickings. Minnowlike lures are best for this occasion.

- **Hunger:** The simplest reason of all. When a bass is hungry, it eats anything resembling food, as would you or I. This is simply survival, and it is the most common reason that bass take lures.

- **Greed:** A smaller bass makes a move toward your lure but a bigger one rushes to grab it instead. Yet when you examine the bass's stomach you find it full of food. The motive wasn't really hunger.

- **Gluttony:** When schooling bass are in a feeding frenzy, I have caught them not only with stomachs distended by food but also with minnows sticking out of their throats. *When food is plentiful,* bass keep gorging.

- **Protective instinct:** While guarding a nest of eggs or a school of fry, a bass will seize a lure and carry it away from the nest without attempting to eat it. This is why a nesting bass is so easy to catch: its protective instinct overrides its normal fear of man.

- **Curiosity:** When a bass follows closely behind your lure but doesn't take it, it's more curious than hungry. By changing lures or suddenly halting the retrieve, often a bass can be enticed into taking a lure.

A large bass is pursuing a giant 12-inch plastic worm, more curious than hungry. Note how the aging process has frayed dorsal and tail fins. Bass this wary may never be caught on artificial lures.

- **Reflexive action:** Even though bass are glutted with food, a lure twitched rapidly over the surface or trolled extra fast can trigger reflexive strikes.

- **Anger:** When you locate a big bass in command of a certain spot, you can goad that bass into striking. Just repeatedly cast into its hang-out until you rouse its ire. This may take several dozen casts and a change of lures.

- **Territorial aggression:** Bass have a pecking order: the bigger the bass, the choicer its lair. Bass aggressively patrol a chosen area and chase away intruders. When your lure intrudes, it attacks.

This lunker bass was lying in ambush on bottom covered with eel grass. It popped up instantly when it caught the vibes of a snorkling photographer. Its sonar-sensing of intruders is its main key to survival.

So with all these reasons why bass take lures, how do we know which to exploit? We don't. But rather than trying to force my choice on them, I follow a simple rule: "Ten casts and change lures." This way I let the *bass* tell me which lure, color, and action *they* want. Try it. It's catching!

3 The Anatomy of a Bass

We know a bass has a brain. Sometimes bass seem smart, while other times they come on as pretty dumb. Countless times during a half-century of matching wits with America's most popular gamefish, these behavorial swings have made me wonder: Just how smart is this breed?

This question especially grabs me when I'm fishing a spot I know has abundant bass, and I've tried all my pet plugs and wily manipulations with nary a pickup. At these times I feel dumber than the bass. So, to smarten up I've spent hours studying, researching, checking lab experiments on bass senses, and querying bass-wise professionals. Here's what I've found out.

First, maybe "smart," at least in the sense we normally use it, isn't the precise word to describe bass intellect. A bass *is* canny and alert, and all its senses are keener than those of humans, except sight. Blind a bass and it will both thrive and survive, whereas a lone, blind human would perish. Using its other senses, a bass can detect our presence at least 100 feet away and will hide until we depart.

To better appreciate these feral "smarts," let's do an appraisal of the bass's physiology. Look at the accompanying sketch detailing the physical senses of a bass. Like human beings, it has sight, hearing, taste, smell, and feel. Let's examine each to assess its importance in a bass's existence and its relationship with anglers.

Sight is our primary sense. Not so with bass. Look at the eye. It's big, bright, and you would think super-sharp since it's on such a superb predator. On the contrary. The next time you catch a bass, lay it flat,

Photograph by Glen Lau.

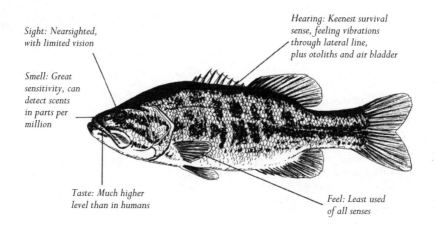

Sight: Nearsighted, with limited vision

Hearing: Keenest survival sense, feeling vibrations through lateral line, plus otoliths and air bladder

Smell: Great sensitivity, can detect scents in parts per million

Taste: Much higher level than in humans

Feel: Least used of all senses

Survival Senses of Largemouth Bass

place your hand over the eye to block the light for a few seconds, then quickly take it away. The iris stays wide open; the burst of light has no effect. Do this to a human eye and the iris quickly contracts to reduce the sudden flood of light.

Like a camera lens, our iris opens or closes to focus on an object to sharpen our vision. But since the bass's iris stays wide open, the fish is myopic, or nearsighted, with limited vision.

Hearing is a bass's keenest survival sense. Without acute hearing a bass would either be eaten young or starve. It has several organs for detecting different kinds of sounds. The most sensitive is the *lateral line,* which runs along both sides of the body and the frontal area around the eyes. Located here are thousands of tiny micropores; in the center of each is a minute nerve ending called a *neuromast.*

These receptors record low-frequency vibrations, fewer than 50 cycles per second, such as those from the fin movements of minnows or the wiggle of an artificial lure. Even in muddy water with near-zero visibility, this sensitive sonar system enables a bass to determine from a moving object's vibrations its shape, speed, and heading as well as a point of interception.

Fish also have an echolocation system for receiving high-frequency sounds of thousands of cycles per second, such as those emanating from rattling hooks on a rapidly vibrating lure or the echo of a lure rapping against wood or rocks. This system detects vibrations using as resonators *otoliths,* or hollow head bones, and an air bladder. (For more on bass and sound, see chapter 13.)

Conclusion: Because the average visibility in bass waters around the nation varies from a few inches to a few feet, *most* of the bass we catch first become aware of our lure's presence through their sense of *hearing,* not sight. Later we'll discuss how to use this knowledge to outfox wily bass.

Taste: Bass have taste buds in the mouth similar to ours, but theirs are much more sensitive, allowing them to accept or reject items by tasting inhaled water. Recent studies reveal that bass show a preference for plastic worms flavored with additives such as crawfish or minnow enzymes. Hard lures can also be dipped in liquid flavors for added appeal.

Do flavors fool wise old bass into taking lures? This is unproven, but it's logical to conclude that once a bass takes a lure, a flavor might make it hold on longer. This is a plus for fishermen, because it gives us more time to set the hook.

Smell is more closely aligned with taste in bass than it is in humans. We reject edibles that smell bad and so do bass, but to a much higher degree. For instance, tests have shown these things to be repulsive to bass, even in minute concentrations: amino acids from our hands, gasoline, motor oil, and tobacco. The presence of these on a lure may explain why one fisherman isn't catching fish while his nonrepulsive partner racks up a good catch of bass.

There are two easy ways to make sure your hand acids don't repel bass. One is to wash them with soap and add a scent such as fish oil or other attractant. Lacking these, try saturating your hands with saliva. It contains a substance called *ptyalin,* an acid neutralizer. Remember that old saw, "Spit on your lure for good luck"? Not a bad idea now that we know about ptyalin!

Feel is probably the least used of the bass's five senses. We know a bass can feel: Touch a bass in a tank and it darts away, and bass respond to physical contact during mating. Little is known about how bass utilize their sense of feel, but as far as fishermen are concerned, it's relatively unimportant.

So how does all this help us outthink sage old bass? Knowing how its senses function, especially its ability to detect underwater vibrations, we can be sneakier in our approaches and choose lures more carefully so that we do more appealing than alerting.

Our first smart offensive move is to do whatever possible to keep the bass's ultrasensitive sonar system from detecting our approach. Beware these sounds and dampen them: outboards, electric motors, oars, foot crunching, water sloshing, anchoring, and tackle box clacks.

Use the anchor more and the electric motor less to maintain casting position. As you approach the hangout you plan to fish, have the anchor suspended just over the bottom so that it can be eased down quietly, with no warning clunks.

Check the water clarity regularly. Here's how: Tie on a white lure, reel it against the rod tip, shove it downward, and note the depth at which it disappears. Beyond 6 feet the water is clear, 2 to 4 feet is average, 1 to 2 feet is cloudy, and just a few inches is turbid. Here are lure colors and tactics that work best under these four visibility conditions.

Clear water: Have ready the lures you plan to use, which will minimize unwanted tackle box noises. Stay as far from the target area as you can cast accurately. Begin by casting to the outer cover with a variety of lures, then the intermediate area, and finally farther back. Try crawling surface lures over and through the heavy stuff, flip the outer pockets, and do it *quietly!*

Select natural patterns such as shiner, crawfish, and perch, choosing actions that most resemble these food fish in motion. Begin with ¼- to ⅝-ounce sizes for larger bass, scaling down if only juveniles are active. Manipulate surface lures gently and slowly to bring bass out of deep hangouts. Use lighter lines, which are harder for bass to detect.

Average water: This is normal habitat in the bass world. Try all colors, sizes, and actions of lures. Try waters from top to bottom, in every possible bass spot, including deep drop-offs, heavy weeds, points, riprap, reefs, and open covers such as lily pads, reeds, and arrowroot. If no bass appear, try lures you don't normally use, such as 12-inch giant worms on top and mini-worms near bottom.

Cloudy water: Think sonar sense and choose lures with vibratory actions so sharp they make your rod tip flutter. Use commotion-making surface lures such as chuggers, wobblers, zigzaggers, and throbbing spinners. Also try extra-noisy buzzbaits fished at a very slow pace. Choose lure colors with more contrast and flash to enhance visibility once the bass gets close enough for a sharp look.

Turbid water: Here a bass relies solely on its sonar sense, so you should choose lures that emit maximum vibrations, or noise, such as rattlers and spinners that activate with slow movements. Work surface lures in one spot long enough to attract bass from extreme distances. Reel crankbaits slowly to help bass identify vibration tracks and determine an interception point.

Color perception is a moot point among both scientists and veteran anglers, but we know that a bass's eye has the same rods and cones that enable humans to distinguish colors. In numerous tank tests, ichthyologists have proven that bass can discern even pastel shades of red, blue, and green.

Many times over the years my fishing partner has had a hot streak catching bass on a certain shade of worm, say light blue. Rather than use his catching color, I first tried all other colors to be certain the bass really were being choosy. In every case I couldn't keep pace until I tied on the exact shade of lure he was using. Thus, just as fly fishermen strive to match the hatch, you should keep changing lure colors until you hit the magical hue of the moment. And remember, it can change with the hours.

In summary, don't think of bass as being smart because you can't catch them when you know they're there. Think of them as wary creatures that have learned to survive in a dangerous world where not detecting a predator means death.

It's your challenge to keep them unaware of your predatory presence. Present lures that look and act like natural forage, but add little tricks of your own that trigger strikes. Strive to learn something of value every trip and keep notes for reminders. And handle the fish with loving care: Every bass you return helps preserve this precious species.

4 Getting a Good Start

I f you're new to bass fishing, you'll find a lifetime of fun, fascination, challenges, and frustrations awaiting you. If you're a seasoned bass angler and have already experienced these things, the following will serve as a refresher course.

One of the larger blessings of bass fishing is that you can't take your troubles with you. There's no time for them; your mind must be at the end of your line where the bass live. To me, bass fishing is the world's only sport where you can watch your troubles run down a line and get lost, fishing for a wonderful, wacky critter called bass.

Bass anglers are united by a common bond. I couldn't begin to count the occasions when being able to talk bass has meant instant camaraderie with doctors, lawyers, clergymen, dentists, plumbers, electricians, airline pilots, new neighbors, and on and on. The results have ranged from personalized service to enduring friendships.

Now let's get started. First, a bit about fishing gear.

METHODS

Spincasting is the most popular rig, used by about 45 percent of American anglers. The reason is simplicity. Spincasting eliminates the troublesome backlashes of baitcasting reels and the snazzles of spinning reels. A spincasting reel has a stationary line spool enclosed in a cone with a small hole through which the line flows. A thumb button controls the line. Spincasting reels are moderately priced and a practical method for beginners, although a lack of line control at the end of the cast means they are less accurate than baitcasting or spinning outfits.

Spinning reels are similar to spincasting reels except that the stationary spool isn't enclosed in a cone. A forefinger against the spool controls the line for distance and accuracy. Spinning takes some getting used to because you cast right-handed and retrieve left-handed, with the reel hung beneath the rod instead of mounted on top of it. Right-hand retrievers are available for those who insist. About 35 percent of all fishermen use spinfishing equipment, mostly because of its versatility in casting baits from ultralights to heavyweights. Spools can be swapped quickly for ones with lighter or heavier lines.

Baitcasting is the oldest method of casting and retrieving lures and the choice of professional bass fishermen for most needs. About 15 percent of sport fishermen use baitcasting rigs. Baitcasting requires more skill than spincasting or spinning and a great deal of practice to become proficient. The biggest problem is backlash, caused by a "dumb thumb" that fails to control the revolving spool. However, modern reels equipped with magnetic or centrifugal brake systems help keep backlashes to a bearable minimum. Baitcasting is my choice for bass fishing because it delivers the most accurate casts and gives better control when battling lunker bass.

Balanced Baitcasting or Spincasting Outfits

Lure Weight	Rod Length	Action	Line Test
¼ – ⅜ ounce	5½ – 6 feet	Light	8 – 12 pounds
⅜ – ½ ounce	6 – 6½ feet	Medium	10 – 14 pounds
½ – ⅞ ounce	6½ – 7 feet	Medium–Heavy	12 – 20 pounds

Balanced Spinning Outfits

Lure Weight	Rod Length	Action	Line Test
¹⁄₂₅ – ³⁄₁₆ ounce	5 – 6 feet	Light	4 – 6 pounds
³⁄₁₆ – ⅜ ounce	6 – 7 feet	Light	8 – 12 pounds
⅜ – ⅝ ounce	7 – 8 feet	Medium	14 – 20 pounds

Here is the author rigged for a day's bass fishing, with four outfits to do it. Three baitcasting rods, a 6-foot with 12-pound line for ¼-ounce lures, a 6½-foot with 15-pound line for ⅓-ounce lures, and a 7-foot with 20-pound line for ½-ounce lures and up. There's also a 5½-foot ultralight spincasting rod with a 6-pound line for ⅒-ounce lures. Each outfit is balanced to easily and accurately cast these four lure classes, which cover the size ranges in the bass's food chain.

Fly fishing is one of the most enjoyable ways to fish, but only about 5 percent of bass anglers fish this way. Fly fishing catches the fewest bass, especially with subsurface flies, but it can be deadly with surface lures such as poppers or bugs on calm waters. A good starter rig is a nine-foot rod, an eight-weight bug-taper floating line, a single-action reel, and a kit of poppers.

LURES AND BAITS

Beginning bass anglers find it mighty bewildering to walk into a modern tackle store and see hundreds of lures in all sorts of designs, shapes, colors, and sizes—all for bass. Where do you start?

Well, you can simplify things by limiting your selection to the dozen lures most often listed by bass fishermen entering *Sports Afield*'s Fishing Awards Program, which I have directed for twenty-five enlightening years. I call these the deadliest dozen and will cover their use in detail in the next chapter. Meanwhile, here's a quick overview of how they work.

Plastic worms are the catchingest of all artificial bass lures—an imitation of a nightcrawler, made of soft polyvinylchloride, that looks, feels, and when scented, even smells and tastes like a big worm. You can rig a worm in many ways, including weedless for use in heavy cover. This makes a plastic worm an ideal beginners' lure because you can cast it anywhere bass live. Working a worm is simple: Just cast it near cover; most strikes occur as it settles. When you feel a tug or unusual tension, reel slack out of the line and set the hook with gusto. Then keep a tight line and enjoy the tussle.

Crankbaits are so named because you just cast them out and crank them back. Their minnowlike bodies have a lip that plows through the water to make them wiggle alluringly. Depending on the size and angle of the lip, crankbaits run from shallow to deep.

Lipless crankbaits, or **vibrators**, are balanced so that they wiggle without needing a lip, using the same principle that makes a flag ripple in a breeze. Cast one close to cover, let it settle to different depths, then retrieve it steadily.

Slim minnows, as the name implies, look like slim minnows floating at rest. Different sizes of lips make them run from shallow to deep when retrieved, but most bass are caught by twitching them on the surface like a dying minnow: cast out, twitch-twitch, then retrieve.

Surface wobblers are floating lures with a big lip that makes them wobble from side to side on a steady retrieve. The Jitterbug is the surface wobbler most often named in bass tournament entries across the nation.

In-line spinners, also called French spinners, have a weighted body with a spinning blade; the Mepps spinner is the outstanding lure of this type. In-line spinners need no tricky retrieve; just cast them out and retrieve just fast enough to turn the blade. This is one of the few bass lures that will catch many species of fish.

Overhead spinners, or **spinnerbaits**, have a weighted head with the spinner blade whirling over a skirted body. This commotion helps bass find the lures, especially when visibility is limited. Cast out a spinnerbait, let it settle, then make a steady retrieve. Try different size lures and spinner blades as well as different colors.

A **jig-and-trailer** is a leadhead hook combined with any soft, eel-shaped body or pork rind. The best way to fish a jig-and-trailer is so *slowly* that it keeps nudging bottom cover all the way back. Stopping to twitch it every third or fourth crank adds additional attraction.

Weedless spoons have a wire weedguard that fends off weeds and snags; you can cast them anywhere without hanging up. According to entries in the *Sports Afield* Awards Program, the Johnson Silver Minnow is by far the most popular weedless spoon. Crawl it over and through surface weeds and bottom covers. A strip of pork rind or a soft plastic frog added to the hook can at times make the lure more effective.

Slab, or **jigging spoons** aren't used that often but they're very effective for bass in deep water. These heavy spoons are designed to reach bottom in 20 to 50 feet of water, where they're jigged up and down to trigger strikes.

Crawfish are the number-one live bait for bass across America. Hook one in the tail with a 3/0 O'Shaughnessy hook, add a couple split-shot to the line, and crawl it slowly over the bottom.

Live minnows are the second-best live bait according to bass fishermen. Minnows vary by region, so check with your local live-bait dealer to see which minnow species and size is most popular in your area.

This is just the bare bones of bass fishing for sometime bass fishermen. By going whenever you can and keeping notes of where and when you catch bass, you'll store bits of lore in your God-given computer that will one day make you the expert you almost are!

Getting Unsnagged

Show me a bass fisherman who rarely gets snagged and I'll show you one who doesn't catch many bass. Getting snagged is just part of placing lures where bass live. And just as this is an art, so too is getting unsnagged.

When your hook grabs something and hangs on, the first thing to do is . . . nothing. Let the line go slack as you assess the situation. If you're hung on a tree limb, for instance, feel the lure through and over the branches using short, gentle twitches of the rod tip. And keep the line slack: tension only makes the hooks hang on firmly. Most of the time, shaking the lure gently with a slack line will disengage the hooks.

If the lure is hung solidly, ease close—*but hold it*: Don't reach for that lure until you check for nearby wasps, hornets, or a snake. If any look belligerent, cut your line, beg their pardons, and continue on your way.

If a lure is snagged on the bottom, most of the time you can push it free with the rod tip. "Plug knockers" are available for disengaging badly snagged plugs from bottom hang-ups. Some folks make their own using an old spark plug.

Keeping Bass to Eat

In areas where heavy fishing pressure has made bass scarce, it's now the custom to release bass for other anglers to enjoy. However, in waters with an abundance of year-class bass from 1 to 2 pounds, there's nothing wrong with keeping a couple of bass for a family meal. This is part of the pleasure in catching bass and a reward for becoming sufficiently skilled to fool them.

Practice Accuracy at Home

Accurate casting gives you a definite edge in bass fishing. There are times when being a foot off target will lose fish that a dead-on cast will catch. Learn to be a dead-on lure caster by practicing at home. Use a bucket or an old tire for a target and a plug with hooks removed. Begin by making short casts at first, then make longer casts as skills develop. Practice until you can drop that plug within a foot of the target most of the time. More hours spent fishing will hone your eye–hand coordination, and soon you'll hold your own with the veterans.

5 Fishing the Deadliest Dozen

H ere are the particulars of the twelve best bass catchers—the deadliest dozen, which we introduced in chapter 4. Try all twelve if you want to spend more time catching bass than just fishing for them. As you review this chapter you'll discover that each lure does a specific job, appeals to bass in a different way, reaches particular bass hangouts the others don't, or especially resembles some critter bass like to eat. I suggest you take this deadly dozen to a swimming pool to practice the techniques and become familiar with the actions of each one.

PLASTIC WORMS

Clearly number one, there is no other lure so specific for a fish species as the plastic worm is for bass. With it a beginner has almost as much chance as a pro of catching a whopper bass. The edge goes to the angler who casts more accurately, learns the waters, and knows when and how to set the hook.

There are many ways to rig and weight a plastic worm, but the universal favorite is Texas style. A 6-inch soft plastic worm is rigged with a 3/0 to 5/0 long-shank hook, in your choice of many designs, buried in the body of the worm to make it weedless. This is what makes this method ideal for beginner and expert alike. A Texas-rigged worm can be cast anywhere a bass lives and retrieved without snagging. A bullet-shaped slide sinker mounted ahead of the hook provides proper casting weight.

plastic worm

Slide sinker weights range from ⅛ ounce through one ounce, with ⅜ ounce being most popular. Some anglers think a ⅛ ounce weight with 6-pound line sinks slower and is more attractive to bass. Others prefer a 15-pound line with a ½-ounce sinker, reasoning that the heavy rig is easier to cast and can boss bigger bass out of thick cover. Some believe a lightweight rig allows a bass to engulf the worm more easily and that the heavier weight tends to obscure the feel of a pickup. Devotees of the heavier weight believe their rig gets to the bottom faster and enables them to get in more casts per hour, thus increasing their chances.

I prefer to straddle the fence and rig two outfits. At certain times of the day in certain covers, the lightweight rig produces; the heavier rig also has its places and moments. I like to let the bass decide by giving them alternate choices throughout the day.

The choice of hook style is a personal thing. There are so many that one is bound to suit your needs. I prefer a 3/0 Mister Twister Keeper Hook, with a barbed arm from the hook eye to secure the worm, keep it from twisting, and make it weedless.

Most anglers use baitcasting, spincasting, or spinning rigs, but some fishermen use a cane pole to fish a plastic worm, weighted with a couple of split-shot and eased quietly into every hole that might hold a bass. This is worm fishing at its simplest, and it can be very effective.

A few words about worm colors. There are so many it can be bewildering to a beginner, but look at the record. In order, the best-selling colors are purple, blue, black, red, brown, and motor oil. Buy some of each, use them all, and let the bass tell you which they prefer at that moment.

How to fish them

As Robert Browning said, "Let me count the ways!" There are too many to list here, but I'll describe the two most popular methods nationwide.

No doubt the Texas rig with a slide sinker catches more bass than all other rigs combined. Cast it into or beside any cover 2 or more feet deep. As the worm alights, keep your rod tip high overhead. You want to let the worm settle to the bottom by lowering the rod tip, always keeping the worm under slight tension. If the line is slack as the worm settles, you can't sense when a bass takes it in. A bass doesn't grab a plastic worm; it sucks it in, just as you used to do with a strand of spaghetti when mom wasn't looking. Only faster.

How fast? I learned by watching a Glen Lau film in slow motion. Film goes through the camera at 24 frames per second. In one frame the bass had its head sticking out of the weeds and my worm settled 15 inches away. In the next frame, less than $\frac{1}{24}$-second later, the worm is

Setting the hook is not a matter of muscle; it's speed in the rod tip. And the best way to attain maximum speed is to use a rod with a long handle and a two-handed set, pulling back with the upper hand and pushing forward with the lower hand. The faster you move the tip, the deeper the hook is buried, and the fewer lost bass.

The best way to ensure that a released bass will survive: Don't touch it; the amino acid on our hands can cause fatal infections. When possible, grip the hook with pliers and gently shake the bass free.

gone and the bass hasn't moved. This means that by the time I felt the minute tug of that worm moving, it was already too late to set the hook!

Much of the time there's no doubt when a bass inhales your worm: there'll be a sharp tug as the line is jerked forward. Other times, the take is so gentle only a super-alert pro can sense it. Just keep your mind at the end of the line, and if the line looks or even hints at feeling different, set the hook with gusto!

To set the hook, point your rod toward the bass and reel in slack until the rod is parallel with the water. With your left hand on the foregrip and your right hand on the butt, quickly pull toward you with the left hand and push away with the right. This is the most effective way to put speed into the rod tip, and speed is what drives the hook home, not brawn. Practice the speed-set at home, letting someone with a glove hold the line, arm hanging limply. You'll be amazed at the effectiveness of the speed-set.

CRANKBAITS

You just cast these plugs out and crank them in; hence the name. Crankbaits come in all shapes and sizes, in both floaters and sinkers, and with various sizes and shapes of lips that make them wiggle and run from barely beneath the surface on down to 35 feet. It pays to acquire an assortment of small, medium, and large crankbaits to match the baitfish bass are feeding on. Just keep changing lures until the bass say you've got it right. As for colors, I prefer natural scale patterns such as shad, shiner, perch, and bluegill, with flashy, metallic backgrounds.

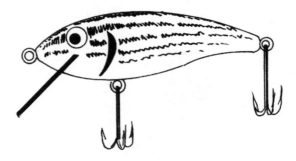

crankbait

A good starter kit includes three different colors in each of the three popular sizes of crankbaits—¼, ⅜, and ½ ounce, in both shallow and deep-running types.

How to fish them

First make short casts and observe the lure closely to find the best retrieve speed. Then just cast it out and reel in at this pace. Occasionally it helps to get tricky. During the retrieve, try speeding it up, slowing it down, even stopping it in order to trigger strikes from tailing bass.

In areas where shorelines drop off sharply, say in 6- to 15-foot depths, add just enough weight to the lure—using SuspenDots or an equivalent—to cause it to sink slowly. Cast close to cover bordering darker, deeper water; let the lure slowly sink until slack line signals you've hit bottom; then begin a very steady retrieve. Pause to twitch the lure at intervals, and be ready to set the hook. Also try trolling at slow and fast speeds along dark weed lines.

LIPLESS CRANKBAITS

This unique family of lures has been around since the early 1950s. A delicate balance between the line-tie and an inner weight begets a sharp, fluttering action much like a live shad. Lipless crankbaits are shaped like the small fish bass feed on and are one of the steadiest catchers, especially for larger bass. The lures come in floaters as well as sinkers, and in sizes from tiny 1/10-ounce lures up to large 1-ounce sizes. Natural colors like shad, shiner, bluegill, and perch are steady producers if you activate them in a manner similar to these same food fish.

Here again, start with three different colors in each of the popular sizes: 1/4, 3/8, and 1/2 ounce.

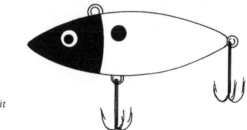

lipless crankbait

How to fish them

This is the ideal plug for "gunning and running," a tactic used to find bass when they're on the move. Just keep casting and moving from one type of cover to another, casting and retrieving from top to bottom, using sizes from tiny to large in a wide range of colors. Cast close to, inside, and around weedy cover such as lily pads, weeds, cattails, brush, and hydrilla. Begin an immediate retrieve varying from slow to fast, intermittently stopping and starting to trigger reflexive strikes from tailing bass.

SLIM MINNOWS

This family of lures looks like the name, a slim minnow. They hit the market in 1962 when the Rapala blowtorched into national prominence after an article in *Life* magazine. The Finnish makers were never able to meet the demand for their handcrafted, balsa-bodied lures. Then the Rebel minnow, made of plastic and easier to cast, came along to help boost this slim-minnow design into lure history.

Slim minnows are mainly floaters (some are very slow sinkers) with varying size lips to make them run from shallow to deep. My tackle box runs the gamut from lures a couple inches long to some more than 6 inches; colors are mostly in natural scale patterns over shiny metallic backgrounds.

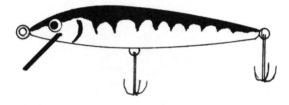

slim minnow

How to fish them

Although these slim lures were designed to dive and swim, most bass are caught by fishing them on top, like an injured, dying minnow. This triggers explosive bass strikes!

Cast one near cover or over weeds and let it lie motionless for as long as you can stand it. Then twitch it just enough to make a gentle slurping noise. Let it lie for a slow ten-count, and repeat. Also, try reeling barely fast enough to cause the lure to make a soft hump in the surface. Detonating!

SURFACE LURES

This broad family of lures is made up of noisemakers, each of which disturbs the surface with its own peculiar commotion. Some have a built-in, self-animating action on retrieve. Others have no action other than that imparted by the skilled workings of the angler.

Of the self-animating types, the standout by far is the Jitterbug, introduced in the mid-1930s and named after a then-popular dance

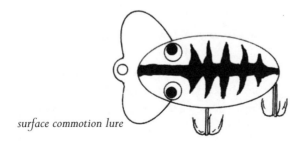

surface commotion lure

Two bass fought over this lure and both got hooked. Not suprising when the lure is a Lucky 13, one of the all-time greats in commotion-type surface lures. It's dead-liest when twitched under to make it gurgle then bob back to the surface.

craze. I recall the lure with a grin because I caught my first two bass over 5 pounds on two successive casts with a Jitterbug. When reeled steadily, its unique headplate causes this lure to waddle from side to side with an audible gurgle-gurgle-gurgle. Another of this self-activating type is the Crazy Crawler, which has two spoon-shaped arms that give it a crazy, rolling, side-to-side crawl stroke. Both of these unusual surface plugs are easy to work in a variety of ways, from slow stop-and-go commotions to steady, noisy retrieves that bring bass out of heavy cover.

Surface lures that have no action other than that imparted by the angler include: 1) chuggers, which have a hollow face and make a chugging sound when twitched sharply; 2) those that dart from side to side when steadily reeled using a reel-reel, twitch-twitch timing, called "walking the dog"; and 3) lures with propeller spinners on head, tail, or both that churn the water to make loud spluttering sounds.

Propeller lures pose one of the mysteries of bass fishing. For some unfathomable reason, there are times when bass prefer one of these three types over the other two, smashing into the chosen one and ignoring the others. So it pays to keep changing types to discover the one that rings their bell.

A final type of surface noisemaker has been around many generations in various designs, but in recent years it has hit the hot list: buzzbaits. These modern versions have oversize double and triple blades with radical curves that amplify surface commotion and sound like a high-speed egg-beater. Occasional bass fishermen ought to use buzzbaits more often; pros rely on them. With all surface lures, colors matter little.

How to fish them

The self-animators seem to produce better when reeled steadily, setting up a repetitious sound sequence. This is especially true in cloudy water or at night, when visibility is low to nonexistent. Beginners especially do well with self-animators because they attract bass from a wide area.

When fishing the chugger-type lure, twitch it just enough to make the hollow head do its thing. Repeat the maneuver several times, from slow to fast, then move on to another spot. The darting types require practice to do the walking-the-dog caper, making the lure head swing from side to side. It's done by delicate timing between rod-tip twitches and quick reel-handle turns. There's something about this sashaying movement that dares a bass to hit!

Lures with spluttering head or tail spinners are the simplest to manipulate. You can reel them slowly, pause and twitch, jerk violently, or keep them coming steadily. Usually, very slow does it.

Fishing buzzbaits requires faith in the lure, so you must stay with it at intervals all day long. Just cast it out and buzz it back for some of bassing's most thrilling strikes!

IN-LINE SPINNERS

These popular lures have a revolving blade on a weighted shaft in line with a rear hook. The blade, which may be a French, Indiana, or Colorado type, spins around the shaft on retrieve, creating commotion and animating the lure's skirted body.

Both in-line spinners and overhead spinners require maintenance to keep them working properly. Some use glass beads as bearings behind propeller spinners, and over time these may get a lime or algae buildup, which slows spinner action. Polish them with steel wool and add a drop of oil for lubrication.

in-line spinner

Some spinner blades are suspended from a clevis, and you need to be sure it doesn't begin binding after banging against rocks or wood. Reshape the clevis with a pair of pliers until it runs freely. Where spinner blades are mounted on a swivel, be sure it is a ball-bearing type to give instant starts and work at slowest speeds. A drop of oil helps any spinner work better. The most popular sizes of in-line spinners are ⅜ and ⅝ ounce.

How to fish them

In-line spinners are the soul of simplicity: just cast them into shore cover and reel back slowly, varying the speed of retrieve and covering the water from top to bottom. When the surface is calm, reel just fast enough to cause the spinner blade to leave a V-wake on the surface. At times this works like magic.

Overhead spinnerbaits are totally unlike other single-unit lures. Among countless bass thus caught, I have yet to catch one with the entire lure in its mouth. It approaches from behind, rolls on its side, and eyeballs the lure.

The bass then opens its mouth, flares its gills, and engulfs only the body of the lure, never the spinner. This is the first sensation of a pickup for the fisherman—usually felt as a lessening in tension on the line or a sudden tug.

When a fisherman sets the hook, the bass closes its jaws and the battle begins. At times a bass mouths only the skirt—this is called "short striking." Adding a single trailer hook will usually catch these wary strikers. Setting the hook twice is a good procedure for better hooking.

OVERHEAD SPINNERBAITS

Overhead spinnerbaits have a weighted head connected to one or more revolving spinners by a V-shaped wire; the line-tie is positioned at the point of the V. The bodies are covered with both plastic and hair skirts, which flutter in the spinner wash and lend a great deal of animation.

spinner bait

How to fish them

Spinnerbaits are more versatile than in-line spinners and can be modified to suit specific requirements. On some you can change the size of the spinner blade to give faster or slower action or more vibration. A larger spinner blade, for instance, will run slower and shallower—good for fishing in and around shallow-water hangouts.

Spinnerbaits work better for fishing deep drop-offs because the heavier bodies cause the overhead spinner to gyrate all the way to the bottom. In-line spinners don't go into motion until pulled in a straight line. This is why in-line spinners are outstanding for stream fishing, where the current activates the spinner so effortlessly.

As for colors, white, yellow, and black are the top three nationally, but chartreuse—both in spinner and body colors—is coming on strong. Black appears to be the color for shallow-water fishing, while lighter colors show better for deep fishing.

JIG AND TRAILERS

Here is another oldie-goodie that has been around for generations but is back with a solid following. This is not an amateur's lure; it requires a very sensitive feel to fish properly. But stay with it and you'll find it not only produces consistently but takes some of the biggest bass around.

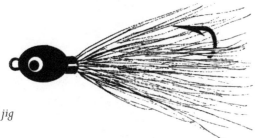

leadhead jig

Jigheads come in all sizes, from tiny ones weighing only ¼₅ ounce up to several ounces. A wide variety of bodies are available: hair, plastic skirts, and many soft-plastic critters such as eels, frogs, salamanders, grubs, crawfish, and minnows. Best colors are naturals, such as white, black, and gray. But sometimes yellow works best!

How to fish them

In a few words: *slowly* and smack-dab on the bottom. Jigheads with hair weed guards can be fished in dense cover. Others can be rigged weed-less by burying the hook in the soft body of a critter lure. A pork-rind frog or eel adds flavor to motion and at times works almost like magic, as do

weedless spoon

plastic baits with added natural flavorings made from crawfish or fish. Keep changing bodies to see if the bass have a periodic favorite.

Keep in mind that this is a do-nothing lure with no action other than that which you apply. So cast, let it sink to the bottom, swim it *slowly* back to you (the slower the better), and set the hook on any suspicious feel.

WEEDLESS SPOONS

One look at this unusual lure leaves little doubt that the first one was fashioned from a tablespoon way back in grandpappy's day. The elongated spoon shape makes it wobble from side to side, and a wire weed guard makes the single hook weedless. You can fish it through the thickest covers and not get hung. The pioneer of all spoons is the weedless Johnson Silver Minnow, and while it comes in a variety of colors, just plain old silver or gold score consistently. Best sizes are ¼ and ½ ounce.

How to fish them

If you're not catching bass in regular covers, they're usually holed up in extra-thick lily pads or shore weeds—ideal territory for the weedless spoon to wobble its way through. Attach a pork frog for added attraction, cast to the back edge of heavy cover, and slowly crawl the spoon back to you.

When you come to an open pocket, give the spoon slack line and let it sink to the bottom momentarily. Hop it into action and slither it all the way back just over the bottom. Also try casting directly into a steep shore and wobbling the spoon down the bottom into deep water. You can also try casting offshore and working the spoon up a sloping bank.

JIGGING SPOONS

These heavyweights have been used in salt water for many years, but only in the past decade have they become popular for bass. It isn't a lure you reach for every day, but when called on it usually comes through. Jigging spoons have thick lead bodies that vary in shape from chunky slabs to slim, minnowlike profiles. The concentrated weight takes them to bottom quickly, as deep as 50 to 75 feet. I like natural shad patterns in ¼, ½, ⅜, ⅝, and 1 ounce.

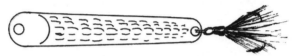

jigging spoon

How to fish them

There are seasonal periods when bass decide to head for deep water. It can happen in both hot and cold weather. If you can't find them in the usual shore covers, it pays to seek them deep, along cliffs, off rocky points, around bridge abutments, or in midlake areas.

Either a sonar unit or a topographical map will show where the deepest spots are, and the best place to begin is on bottom. Natural-color spoons seem to produce best. The deeper the water, the heavier the spoon you'll need. When slack line tells you it has reached bottom, raise the rod tip and jig the spoon up and down. Make five cranks, jig it, five more cranks, jig it—all the way up to locate suspended bass at all levels.

MINNOWS

Skilled guides who pursue bass every day have no doubts: big minnows are the deadliest way to catch big bass. The best minnows are shiners and the various shads, in 3- to 5-inch sizes. Buy locally favored species at local bait stores and keep them lively.

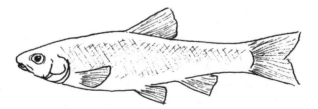

minnow

How to fish them

Here are three good ways to fish minnows: 1) Hook a minnow through the tail with a 2/0 Eagle Claw hook. Keep casting it close to dense, floating cover until the minnow runs back underneath, where the big bass hide. 2) Hook a minnow through both lips and add a couple of split-shot to sink it, then drift with the wind or troll slowly along deep drop-offs. 3) Find weedy shore cover and hook a minnow through the back of its dorsal fin. Inflate a balloon to tennis ball size and half-hitch it to the line a couple of feet above the minnow. Lob the minnow close to dense shore weeds; the minnow will swim back underneath the cover. When a bass grabs the minnow and takes off, the balloon will slide up the line and won't snag on cover.

When a bass takes a minnow, don't set the hook until you feel a strong, steady pull. Then set the hook sharply against a taut line.

CRAWFISH

Next to minnows, these crustaceans are a bass's favorite food. You can seine your own or find them at local bait stores. During my "kid days," we caught crawfish using a tough chicken neck tied to a piece of string. They'll hold on long enough to be grabbed just below the surface. Crawfish can be kept lively in a minnow bucket filled with wet sphagnum moss (available from garden-supply stores).

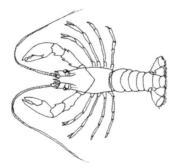

crawfish

How to fish them

Using a long-shank jighead hook, push the barb through the middle of the crawfish's tail, then bury it in the body. It will settle naturally to the bottom where it should be crawled backward in short spurts. Fish it

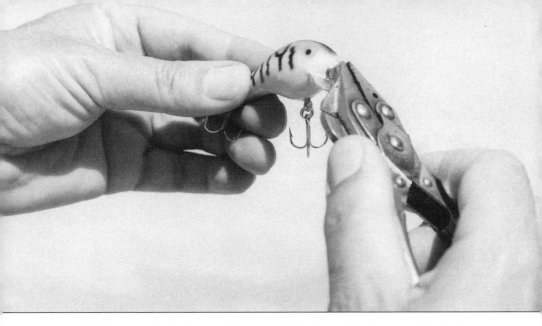

The line-tie is the focal point of lure control. Bending it left of center will make the lure run to the left, to the right vice versa. Bend the line-tie upward and the lure has a tighter wiggle; bend downward to give a wider wobbling action. Use long-nose pliers—and easy does it!

around weeds, over bottom on rocky shores, or along offshore reefs. When you feel a pickup, count three, then set the hook.

Looking back over our deadliest dozen bass lures, I recall some additional points. When you stock your tackle box, keep things together, neatly arranged in trays and categorized as to types, sizes, and colors.

Have at least two in each of the popular colors in case you lose one. When a particular lure stays hot over time, buy a couple of spares for backups. But remember this: Just because new lures are the same model and color doesn't mean they'll wiggle with the same seductive vibes. Numerous things can make a new lure different from your old one: slightly heavier hooks, an extra coat of paint, a line-tie slightly off center or out of sync. So do this.

Take the old and new lures to a swimming pool, along with a pair of long-nose pliers. Cast the old lure first and fix its bass-catching action in your mind. Now look over the new lure's action. Suppose it has a wider wiggle than the old one. Bend the line-tie slightly upward until the two actions match. To give any lure a wider wiggle, bend the line-tie down. Now you have a backup lure you can fish with confidence. Go forth and fish your deadly dozen and become the star you are!

6 Ties That Bind, Knots to Know

W hen a whopper bass pops your line at the knot, nothing says "you're a knothead" so eloquently as that little curl where the knot unraveled. Let's see if we can prevent that from happening to you.

What really causes some knots to break easily while others are stronger than the line itself? To find out, I've stared at knots through a magnifying glass until my eyes crossed, fascinated at what takes place at the moment of fracture.

First, let's examine the world's weakest knot—the simple overhand knot. This knot will break at about 50 percent of the line's given strength: i.e., a 10-pound line will break at 5 pounds. *Never* tie an overhand knot in the main line, especially if the line tests 25 pounds or less. And remember, sometimes overhand knots find ways to tie themselves in the line. The lighter the line, the more critical the presence of an overhand knot becomes.

Before launching into knots themselves, let's examine the properties of fishing lines from early days until now. For comparison we'll list each material as pounds-test-per-square-inch (psi) of line diameter. For a benchmark, let's remember that a strand of spider web tests at 200,000 pounds per square inch.

The earliest line material was braided horsehair, which tested up to 40,000 pounds per square inch. Later came braided silk lines at 60,000 psi. In the 1930s, along came extruded nylon monofilament, to up the level to 100,000 psi. Monofilament held sway for more than a half century, until the last couple of years, when an entirely new concept came along: lines braided from tiny gel-spun polyethylene fibers.

How strong are these new superbraids? Well, humankind has finally matched the spider—about 200,000 pounds per square inch. And rumor has it that new materials and braiding processes are being researched that scale upwards of 500,000 psi.

What does all this mean to fishermen? Compared with nylon monofilament, the new fused lines are about two-thirds smaller in diameter for the same pound test. For instance, a rough measurement used over the years by fishermen is one thousandth of an inch (.001) diameter for each pound test. This means a 30-pound line would measure about .030. But one of the new 30-pound fused lines measures only about .006 in diameter. Moreover, it will stretch only about 3 percent over its length whereas monofilament nylon will stretch about 30 percent. So with the fused superbraids, the serious angler has a super-strong line with a much smaller diameter that bass can't see as well. And the minimal stretch means the knots will be much stronger and it'll be easier to set the hook, particularly at long distances.

While the super-slippery braids have posed problems in knot tying, with inexplicable break-offs at times, this is virtually eliminated in the newer fused lines; these are made up of multiple filaments bonded together, not braided.

I find the fused line reacts to knot tying about like monofilament, so it's worthwhile to discuss what happens when an ordinarily dependable knot breaks and loses you a whopper bass. The glitch happened right after you tied the knot and tightened the folds. Let me suggest a simple demonstration to illustrate, so you'll have it clearly in mind.

Hold your hand at arm's length in front of your eyes. Straighten your fingers and thumb so they fit tightly against each other. This is how the strands of line should look in a knot that draws down properly after you tie it.

Now, insert your thumb between the index and middle fingers and make a fist. This is what happens to strands of line when they don't stay aligned during the draw-down, or tightening, process. That strand of line represented by your thumb will cut through the forefinger strand, and *pop* goes your knot.

Here are the keys to tying strong knots, whichever your pet knot might be:

- Tie it slowly with parallel wraps.

- Tighten it gradually, keeping the strands parallel.

- Draw it down firmly to prevent later slippage.

Now, let's talk about knots that will hold that behemoth bass you hope to catch. And let's begin with old-time favorites that still are popular today because they're simple and reliable.

EYE KNOTS

These knots are for tying to the eye of a hook, swivel, snap swivel, or line-tie of a lure. They are specially selected from dozens of known knots because they can be tied in less than 30 seconds, and they're stronger than similar knots—the ones I didn't choose.

Improved clinch knot

This is the most popular knot among American fishermen—possibly because it's one of the oldest and can be easily tied even with cold fingers. It consistently breaks at about 90 percent of line test. Here are the easy steps for tying it.

Improved Clinch
Run the tag end through the eye of the swivel or hook. Make five turns around the main line. Thread the tag end through the eye loop, then through the main loop. Moisten, then tighten slowly by pulling on the main line and swivel. This is how the finished knot should look, with strands lying parallel, not overlapping.

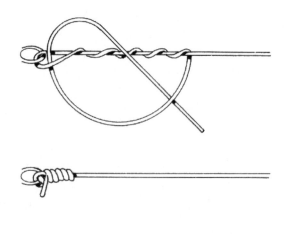

Palomar knot

Chet Palomar noodled out a durable, easy-to-tie knot here. And it checks out at 90 to 95 percent of the line test. Remember to avoid twisting or overlapping the strands as you proceed, making sure they lie parallel like those fingers you looked at. (If you didn't, go back, do what it says, and you'll be a wiser knothead!)

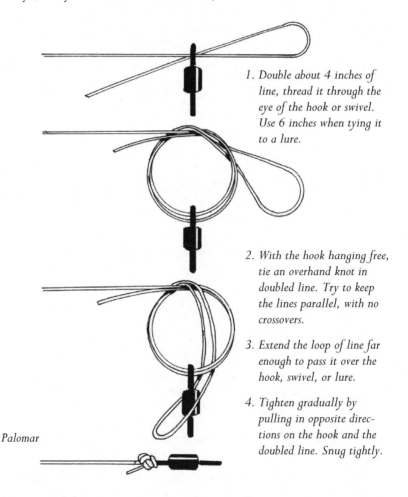

Palomar

1. Double about 4 inches of line, thread it through the eye of the hook or swivel. Use 6 inches when tying it to a lure.

2. With the hook hanging free, tie an overhand knot in doubled line. Try to keep the lines parallel, with no crossovers.

3. Extend the loop of line far enough to pass it over the hook, swivel, or lure.

4. Tighten gradually by pulling in opposite directions on the hook and the doubled line. Snug tightly.

The next two knots are paragons because they're excellent performers and relatively easy to tie, but each takes a bit of getting used to. Once your fingers "remember" the moves, all knots are easy.

Brinson knot

Guide Billy Brinson, of Santee-Cooper country in South Carolina, fashioned this remarkable knot while recuperating from a back injury. I watched this knot break every knot a group of pros tied against it. Very impressive!

Not only does the Brinson knot prove stronger than the line at least 75 percent of the time in strength tests on my Amitex force gauge, but it's the only knot that won't lie to you. In all other knots I've examined under magnification, it's impossible to tell if any have a concealed crossover wrap to weaken them. Not the Brinson. When you tighten this knot, if it has a concealed crossover wrap it will break immediately. When it draws down properly, it will slide together neatly and test 99 percent of line strength.

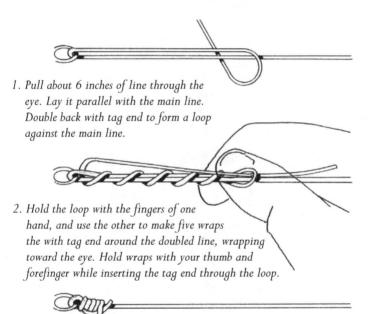

1. *Pull about 6 inches of line through the eye. Lay it parallel with the main line. Double back with tag end to form a loop against the main line.*

2. *Hold the loop with the fingers of one hand, and use the other to make five wraps the with tag end around the doubled line, wrapping toward the eye. Hold wraps with your thumb and forefinger while inserting the tag end through the loop.*

3. *Pull on the tag end to tighten the wraps slightly. Release the tag end, pull the main line and the eye in opposite directions. When the knot elongates suddenly, you'll know it's virtually a 100 percent knot. If it misfolds, this honest knot will break easily to warn you to tie it again, correctly.*

Brinson

Uncle Homer knot

The TV fare was very humdrum one evening, so I spent several hours devising a new knot. My goal was to come up with a knot that would be easy to tie, have minimal foldover tendencies, and be almost as strong as the line. It took me all evening, but I retired at midnight with a feeling of accomplishment.

This one's slightly more involved than other knots, but it's easy once your fingers memorize it. It checks out 99 percent-plus, meaning that most of the time on my force gauge it broke the line, not the knot. So try the Uncle Homer knot. It could become your favorite.

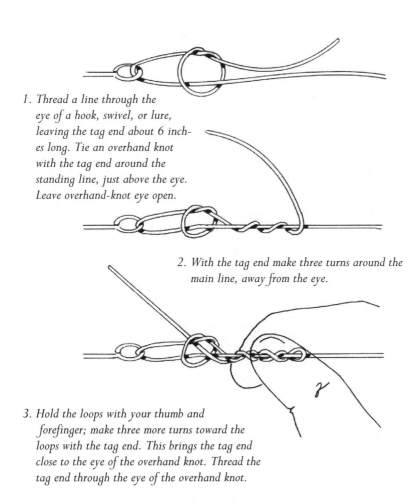

1. Thread a line through the eye of a hook, swivel, or lure, leaving the tag end about 6 inches long. Tie an overhand knot with the tag end around the standing line, just above the eye. Leave overhand-knot eye open.

2. With the tag end make three turns around the main line, away from the eye.

3. Hold the loops with your thumb and forefinger; make three more turns toward the loops with the tag end. This brings the tag end close to the eye of the overhand knot. Thread the tag end through the eye of the overhand knot.

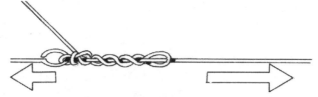

4. *Pull the ends of the line in opposite directions to snug the overhand knot tightly against the lure, hook, or swivel. Leave the tag end loose for the moment.*

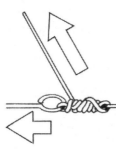

5. *Pull the tag end and the main line in opposite directions, drawing two layers of wraps into a neat spiral. Pull as tightly as possible. This knot comes as close to perfection as any I have tested on a tensiometer.*

Uncle Homer Knot

So much for eye knots. One of the above is bound to suit your needs. You can best determine which one is for you by tying each one until you memorize the moves, and try this simple knot test: Get two weedless spoons from your tackle box and 2 feet of 8-pound-test line. To the eye of one spoon tie your pet knot; to the other end tie the sketched knots. Then wrap a hanky around each spoon and pull in opposite directions to see which knot breaks all the others. That's the knot to adopt, one you can fish with certainty.

Just one observation: All of the above knots are extra strong. If one breaks quicker than it should, it could have folded over improperly. So tie it again, more carefully, and retest it.

Now, let's discuss some non-eye knots, which are bound to come in handy for your angling needs.

KNOTS FOR JOINING LINES

At times it's necessary to join line to line or leader to line. The resulting knot needs to be minimal in size, tapered at both ends to flow through rod guides without bumping, and nearly as strong as the line itself.

Perhaps you want to tie a monofilament leader to your braided line to make it less visible next to the lure. Or perhaps you want to use backing on your reel to save line cost and need to join it to the main line. One of the knots below will be just what you want.

Joiner knot

This knot is a trifle complex the first few times you try it, but hang with it until your fingers remember the moves. Not only is it strong but, when you tighten it, both ends of the knot are neatly tapered for smooth casting.

1. Join the ends of the two lines by tying an overhand knot.

2. Form a loop that stands above the knotted ends.

3. Make six foldovers with lapped lines, keeping the center loop open.

4. Insert the overhand knot through the center loop, pull on each section of the main line, and draw the knot tightly until it tapers at both ends.

5. Clip the ends close to the knot. They will not slip as a blood knot sometimes does.

Blood knot

This is an old favorite of fly fishermen for tying tapered leaders and for joining lines of equal diameter. It's also handy for mending line breaks or for tying new line to backing on a reel.

Lay the ends of the two lines together, paralleling about 6 inches. Hold the loops in the middle and make at least three turns with each tag end. Insert both tag ends through the middle loop. Draw down by alternately pulling on the tag ends and the main line until tightly snugged.

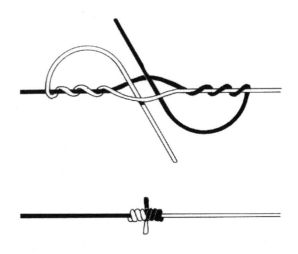

Cut off the tag ends close to the knot. This is how a finished blood knot should look.

Blood Knot

Surgeon's knot

This knot is better for tying together lines of unequal diameter, such as when adding a 30-pound shock leader to a 10-pound fishing line for catching rough-mouthed fish or fishing in abrasive cover such as timber, brush, or craggy rocks.

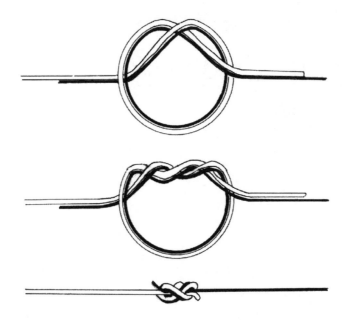

Surgeon's Knot
Place the leader and the line parallel about 6 inches and tie a double overhand knot by making two passes through the eye. Hold both strands on each side of double overhand, moisten, and pull in opposite directions to tighten.

7 Seasonal Tactics for Bass All Year

Mother Nature works her seasonal changes in the bass's world just as she does in ours. Like the weather, bass-catching tactics change with the seasons. All experts have their favorite spring, summer, fall, and winter patterns, depending on where and how they fish. If you have no favorites of your own, Uncle Homer is glad to share his.

Patterns do vary with individuals, but there is a common thread running through their approaches that usually boils down to answering two basic questions: Where are the bass living? And which lures will reach and catch them? This is true whether you live in the far north or the deep south, so let's break it down by seasons. I suggest you make a copy of these pages and take it along for those days when bass seem to be in Nowheresville.

SPRING

We really need to think of spring as three separate timetables: before spawn, during spawn, and after spawn. Bass behave very differently during each of these three periods.

Before spawn

Waters that warm gradually and slowly can produce some very hot fishing. If waters warm rapidly, however, bass forget feeding and devote their time to the stronger urge, spawning. So get out there early and stay with it over shallow flats, backwaters, stump areas, rocky shores, stream mouths, and shallow island perimeters.

Remember, in colder water the bass's reactions are slower. Try these three tactics:

- Weighted spinners retrieved just under the surface so that the spinner humps the water

- Big floating-diving lures reeled slowly but steadily so that they make a V in the surface

- Plastic worms and jigs nudging bottom

During spawn

Waters have warmed enough to turn the basses' thoughts to making love. They don't feed during this period; instead of bashing lures they simply seize and eject them from the nests. You must stay alert to detect pickups.

Try hopping worms over shallow areas, ditto with spinners. Quick motions provoke strikes. Reel deep-running lures until they hit bottom, then stop. This attack attitude will provoke vicious strikes.

After spawn

Spent from spawning, the bigger female bass move into deep holes under dense cover to recuperate. Smaller males zealously guard the spawn to keep packs of bluegills from gobbling down the eggs.

The prime fishing time is from five to six weeks after spawning. The brood is now on its own, the whopper females are back in action, and the males are again feeding after a long layoff.

Because hungry bass eat small bass, possibly some of their own kids, a bass-pattern crankbait is a natural. Retrieve steadily around shore covers. Spinner lures with minnow-shaped bodies worked slowly over the bottom are excellent, especially in dingy water. Also try slim minnow types twitched on the surface and reeled under by gradually speeding up the retrieve.

SUMMER

With the confusion and exhaustion of spawning well behind them, bass are on the prowl for food to replenish their energy reserves, back in

A double on bass: a highpoint in a day's fishing with old friend Doug Hannon, big bass specialist. Although usually a happenstance, doubles can be deliberate if an angler who gets the first strike sets the hook and waits until his partner casts into the same spot.

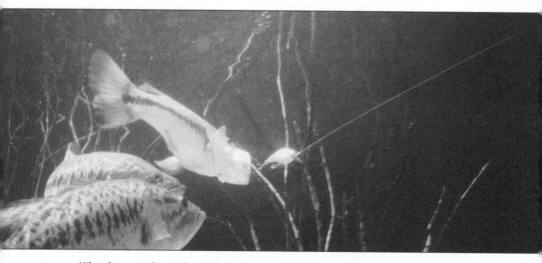

When bass are clustered and one strikes a lure, others usually will follow suit.

their usual haunts, and playing their roles as consummate predators. In short, sic 'em! A lake should be at its peak of production, and bass are on the move gorging on the fingerlings of many species. But bass are individualistic. Some stay in one hangout while others may roam for miles. The key is to keep moving until you locate feeding bass.

I like to set up three baitcasting rigs so that I'm always armed and ready to fire. One reel is spooled with 6-pound monofilament on a light-action rod for small lures in the ¼-ounce class. The second rig has 14-pound line and a medium-light rod for lures in the ⅓-ounce range. The third outfit has 20-pound line and a medium-heavy rod for lures ½ ounce and up.

The light rod is rigged with a ⅛-ounce jighead with a white or yellow grub body. The medium-light rig has a floating-diving crankbait in a natural pattern. The heavy outfit is rigged with a 6-inch purple plastic worm with a ¼-ounce slide sinker. Thus armed, I am ready for fishing all bass habitats from top to bottom, using lures with varied actions for maximum bass appeal.

Usually I'm afloat or afoot at dawn's first light, peppering a shoreline with the floating-diving lure, easing it into every cover nook that catches my eye. A couple of twitches on the surface to get attention, then I scat it under and keep it coming. If ten casts get no action, I switch to a noisy surface lure or a weighted spinner.

If there is still no action, next comes the 6-inch plastic worm, Texas-rigged so it can be cast into cover and come through 90 percent of the time. Cast it anywhere a bass might be and some places it shouldn't be. If one color doesn't produce after ten casts, change to another then another, until bass happen.

Then there are those days when bass are picky. Tempt them with the smaller lures and lighter line, especially if the water is very clear. The lighter line not only is less visible but it also enhances the action of smaller lures.

Rarely does the smaller-lure tactic fail to produce bass. They may be smaller, say in the 1- to 2-pound class, but they're still fun to catch. Keep moving until you cross paths with larger bass.

As the sun climbs higher and lights up the shallow shore hangouts, bass move to deeper, darker habitat. Often this means dense weeds or offshore humps in deep water. For dense weeds try a weedless spoon with a pork-rind trailer. Fish it shallow and deep, fast and slow.

Around the deeper offshore humps, try leadhead jigs with grub bodies, weighted spinners, deep-diving crankbaits, and plastic worms. Cover the darker areas from top to bottom. If an hour's fishing doesn't produce bass, try trolling a deep-running crankbait outside deep shorelines.

When evening shadows sneak slowly onto the scene, return to the early-morning pattern. Now is when bass move toward shore because minnows and insects usually have a late-day activity spurt. Be sure to spend an occasional hour after dark using noisy surface lures off deep, rocky points.

FALL

Autumn means gradually cooling waters around shallower shore-lines, bringing bigger bass back to these now-comfortable haunts to feed heavily and lay up fat for the winter. Scan the waters for a monster bass swirling after minnows or chasing away an intruder.

But remember, a big bass is a wiser bass and alert to any man-made sounds. If you can approach from upwind and ease within casting distance, do so. Have the anchor suspended over the bottom and make no boat noises to spook your quarry.

If the bass is in deep cover, such as lily pads or weeds, use a weed-less spoon with a curlytail worm trailer. Also try a 12-inch floating plastic worm with no added weight (it'll be heavy enough to cast). Twitch it teasingly over the surface.

If that bass you spied moved in spurts, as if chasing minnows, use a lipless crankbait with a shad or shiner finish. Reel it quickly, in short dashes, as if it were scared scaleless that it might get clobbered. And it will!

Also try a floating surface lure cast way beyond the bass, and keep it coming slow and easy, as if it were too dumb to be scared. Stop it dead still near the bass, then twitch it gently. POW!

The urge to fatten up for winter combined with decreased food availability at this time of year can produce some wild feeding forays. So keep moving, watching, and trying every lure in your tackle box to find the magic action, color, size, or depth that lights the bass's fuse. When action is slow, keep moving and questing, and enjoy the colorful autumn panorama all around you.

WINTER

In the north, where winter comes on with a vengeance, there is a magical period, short but sweet—if the timing goes well. It's called "turnover time," and wise old-timers watch for it. Turnover is caused by heavy water. You see, water is heaviest at 39.2°F. And when cold winds pound waves against shorelines, the warm surface waters cool and become heavy enough to sink beneath the warmer, lighter waters beneath. This warms the surface all over the lake—literally turning it over. All aquatic critters sense this significant change.

A lake's entire ecosystem now adjusts itself for the big deep-freeze ahead. Bass move into areas where they'll winter, and with food scarce, you'd expect them to chew up anything edible. Unfortunately, it doesn't work that way. Bass are thinking more of conserving whatever body reserves they've built up for winter's long layover, so movements are held to a minimum. But there are ways to make the most of this challenging period.

The key is to think deep. Bass collect around the deepest drop-offs, midlake holes, old creek channels, bluffs, railroad trestles, and cliffs off very deep points. These are the spots to concentrate fishing. Vertical presentations are the key, and while this can be tedious fishing, it can also be sensational when you ferret out a honey hole. Here's how you go about it.

Select a jighead grub, hair jig, or a slab spoon, and use at least a 20-pound line because you might hook into some monster bass. A sonar is useful to pinpoint these deep holes, preferably where there's an abrupt change in bottom structure, such as a ledge, creek channel, or a flooded escarpment. Don't use an anchor as it might spook a wise old lunker, and don't run the outboard or trolling motor any more than necessary.

Lower the lure until slack line says it's on bottom. Raise the rod tip to gain control of the lure and begin yo-yoing it up and down to give it an undulating rhythm. Occasionally give it a sharp upward sweep, then drop the rod tip quickly so the lure darts toward bottom.

Don't expect a hard strike. Bigger bass rarely take the lure hard enough to jerk the line. What you'll feel is a loosening or tightening of the line tension. At the slightest hint of any change, set the hook. Keep moving and probing bottom holes until you find a gathering spot.

Remember that the four seasons take a continuity of effort, fishing regularly to maintain a feel of where the bass are hanging out. You'll learn to change your fishing patterns with the seasons, and by year's end you'll be thinking more like a bass. You'll also know the feel of becoming a seasoned bass angler, a very special attainment.

8 Where Monster Bass Live

o catch the bass of your lifetime you need to know the special hangouts where these behemoths live. Those in the know catch their
share every year. So can you, but you've got to know how to recognize
these hawg heavens. Some are easily identified but others are difficult to
describe with words alone. Just study the accompanying illustrations;
everything's right there.

Make copies and, as you pursue bass, especially on new waters,
take the illustrations along to help you find each type in the waters you
fish. Once you uncork a dozen or so, you've got yourself a pattern for
finding whopper bass. And you could catch more in one season than most
anglers catch in a lifetime.

Here's a smart tactic: Take along a pocket-size notepad on every
trip. Give a name to each haven where you catch bass, such as Big Bass
Bayou, Ol' Lunker Hole, Hog Hollow, Peckerwood Point, etc. Thus
named, they can be identified more easily, especially if you go regularly
with a fishin' buddy who is as tetched as you are about catching big bass.

Returning to a midlake hangout you've discovered can be difficult
unless you use a system such as triangulation. Here's how to go about it.

As you sit on the spot, look toward shore and find a prominent
short object with a taller object in line and behind it. Do the same thing
90 degrees from the first two. Draw a sketch of these objects in your
notebook and you'll be able to return to the same spot on future trips.

Also, carry along a topographical map of the waters you're on.
These maps show bottom contours and depths, old roadbeds, etc., and

Fred Kesting, executive editor of Sports Afield, *with a 14-pound-plus bass, the largest I've seen caught. She came from deep water as shown by the bulgy eyes, was quickly landed, hand aerated until she could swim away, and lives on. Many anglers would have had this trophy mounted, but Fred declined, saying, "I have the memory mounted in my mind, that'll do it!" Note: This monster fell for a ¼-ounce leadhead jig adorned with a 4-inch plastic worm. Dainty dining for such a gigantic lady!*

are available at your county engineer's office or at many sporting goods stores. You can also order them directly. To order topographic maps you must first obtain an index, and then request maps by name and series. If you are not certain which maps to order, write for a free index to: USGS Information Center, Box 25286, Denver, CO 80225.

After you acquire your map, check with your lake authority to determine the current lake elevation. Write this on your map so that you can compute the true depths when you go fishing.

THE FIFTEEN BEST LAKE HANGOUTS

Now let's examine those big bass hangouts, any one of which could bring heaven a little closer on your very next outing. Remember, Uncle Homer is with you all the way!

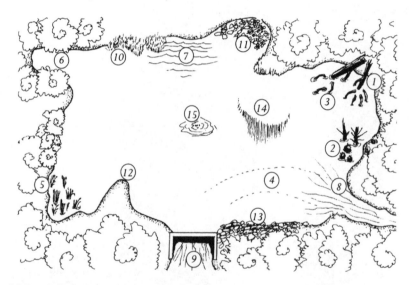

15 Best Lake Hangouts: 1. shore brush, bushes; 2. stumps, standing timber; 3. fallen trees, logs; 4. old creek channels, road beds; 5. stickups; 6. openings in brush and timber; 7. fish the windy side; 8. outside bend of creeks, rivers; 9. below dams; 10. weedbed margins; 11. lily pad concentrations; 12. potent points; 13. rocky shorelines; 14. shoals and reefs; 15. spring holes.

Shore brush, bushes

These are nature's gathering places for insects and the small aquatic creatures on which small fishes feed—and the big bass that feed on the small

Shore brush is a monster-bass hangout because minnows take shelter there; bass stay close by, waiting for one to venture outside. Big bass also hide inside heavy brush, ready to ambush a passing small fish of any kind. Try both surface and diving lures in various sizes.

fishes. Accuracy is a big part of catching bass here. Many days a lazy, canny bass will ignore a lure landing a foot from the brush's edge. But a lure dropped tightly against the edge of a cover line, or barely in it and twitched free as if trying to escape, can be more than ol' Bucketmouth can stand. So practice accuracy.

Approach each spot quietly, and as your lure touches down, watch for brush movement caused by the thrust of a big bass's tail as it moves out to examine your lure. If it doesn't take the lure, keep changing lures and making soft presentations until you discover the one the bass buys. Suggested brush lures are plastic worms, surface-commotion types, floater-divers, crankbaits, weedless spoons, and weighted spinners.

Stumps, standing timber

Big bass lurk around stumps and tree trunks, where they not only hide but also use nature's gift of camouflage. Bass can change body color patterns to match the drab shadows of their backgrounds. As a bass lies motionless it becomes virtually invisible, and a passing minnow makes an easy meal. Keep this in mind as you work your lure magic on bass. Begin with a slim minnow floater and cast beyond timber. Retrieve it fast, just under the surface, staying close to the timber—as if it's scared it might get eaten.

Next try a chugger cast close to a stump. Chug it one time, let it lie for a slow ten-count, then chug gently again. Now twitch it lightly, making it nod its head all the way back. Next, try a buzzbait cast beyond and buzzed past timber. Finally, try a giant 12-inch plastic worm with just enough split shot to slowly sink it. Cast close to the timber, let it settle to the bottom, twitch lightly about once every minute. Awesome!

Fallen trees, logs

When an old tree gives up and falls into a lake or stream, it may be a loss to the forest but it's a boon for bass fishermen. Fish these areas repeatedly and learn their payoff spots; each will be different.

Always fish the shady side first; most likely that's where a lurking bass will hole up. Try this deadly tactic, called "slow rolling a spinner." Tie on a spinnerbait and cast to the back of a fallen tree or log. Remember, a spinnerbait is virtually snagless. Make it crawl up one side of the tree, over the top, then ease it down the other side. Very tempting!

Next, try a weedless spoon with a pork frog, wobbled just over the bottom along both sides of trees and logs. If you have no luck, try a lead-head jig with a soft plastic crawfish; twitch it backward, letting it butt against the timber.

Still no luck? Try a large slim minnow, between 4 and 5 inches long, with maximum buoyancy. Cast past any timber and reel it slowly near, then stop, twitch twitch; reel a couple of feet, stop, twitch twitch; then hurry it back. Be ready for a vicious strike.

Old creek channels, roadbeds

Fishing these is an art best learned through observation. Drive along country roads and walk the courses of creeks. Study the treetops that border each. Notice the pattern made as they follow the bends, stretches, fishhook turns, etc. Keep these patterns in mind as you fish reservoirs that have filled to a depth where the water almost covers the trees. Staying between the tree lines, fish bottom-nudging lures over these flooded creek channels and former roads. Their hard surfaces make them ideal spawning grounds in the spring and good foraging spots year-round.

Especially good for these areas are deep-diving crankbaits weighted to float vertically, so that the large body hides the two treble hooks on the belly. It's amazing how you can cast these past trees and never get hung up as the wiggling crankbait bulldozes its way through the branches. Also try Texas-rigged plastic worms hopped over hard bottoms, plus spinners, weedless spoons, and leadhead jigs with plastic tube bodies.

Stickups

Ask native bass fishermen where they catch bass and some will reply, "I just fished the stickups." This is an apt description. Stickups can be weed tips, tops of brush, remains of dead trees, and debris piled up by high water. All indicate places where bass hang out. Even the smallest stickup may be the tip-top of a large mass of roots or brush below. So don't pass by any stickups, no matter how insignificant they may appear above water.

As you move along fishing, keep your eyes constantly sweeping the water ahead for any type of cover immediately below the surface, especially after heavy rains have raised lake levels. These will be stickups when water levels return to normal.

Cast a plastic worm beyond a stickup, let it settle for a five-count, then retrieve it slowly past the stickup. Cast again, let it settle for a seven-count, retrieve. And again, for a nine-count, and retrieve. This way you'll reach bass that are stratified for whatever reason. Also try crankbaits, spinners, and spoons.

Openings in brush and timber

These places are natural cruising grounds for mobile bass that cover a regular course each day. Here's how to recognize them.

When fishing around brushy or timbered areas, approach very cautiously any places where the cover parts to form a lane, slot, or opening in fairly deep water. We call these bass alleys or hog wallows, natural places for big bass to feed.

Cast to the back end of each opening using sinking lures such as plastic worms, jig-and-trailers, spinners, crankbaits, and lipless vibrators. Cover the middle and both sides. If the water is calm, work both sides of the slot with noisy surface lures. When you catch the first bass, quietly ease down the anchor and fish the entire area thoroughly. Remember that big bass like big food, so try your largest lures here.

Once you catch a second big bass from one of these places, you have uncovered a door to hog heaven, because other big bass will take over such an area when it becomes vacant. Share these spots only with your best bassin' buddy; they're special.

The windy side

It's human nature not to fight the wind, so most fishermen head for the calm side of a lake, bay, or river. But bass are usually on the windy side, so unless the wind is so strong that you feel unsafe, that's where you should fish.

Not only is it much easier to cast with the wind than trying to fight it, but also your bass-catching chances are much greater. The breeze blows insects and algae into the water's edge, small fishes assemble to feed on these tidbits, and bass come to feed on them. Try a variety of smaller lures and work them methodically along the shore covers. Soft-body jigs, in-line spinners and overhead spinnerbaits, small crankbaits that resemble minnows, and chugging types are all ideal here.

Keep moving and offering a smorgasbord of lures until you connect with some feeding bass. If the bass aren't on shore cover, they may have fed and gone on to deeper water. Begin working deeper water parallel with the shore, using plastic worms with ½-ounce slide sinkers, casting slightly into the wind and combing bottom all the way back.

Outside bends of creeks and rivers

As any canny stream fisherman knows, where the current flows the food goes—and so do the bass. When you first approach a flowage, take time to study it. Notice how the current boils over a fast run and then heads toward the outside bend. The steady current pressure will undercut that bank, and these undercuts are a haven for bigger bass because they offer cool shade, shelter from the current, and ambush spots for feeding.

The trick is to choose lures that can be worked into the undercuts. If you can anchor your boat in the right spot above the target area, do so. If this is impossible, beach the boat and fish the run on foot.

Use diving crankbaits that can be held tightly against the undercut as they're retrieved. Try lures with small to large lips to cover the run from top to bottom. Also try heavier in-line spinners with frog or tad-pole trailers. Smaller baits are usually better here. Keep changing lure colors and types until you find the key to that undercut.

Below dams

This area is a giant, turbulent fish bowl for many species. Small fishes washed over the spillway or ground up and spit out by the turbines make easy pickings for big, lazy bass that just hang there, waiting for the current to wash these snacks their way.

One way to fish a tailrace is to motor as close to the dam as is safe or permissible, and drift-fish downstream until you run out of deep water. Another is to anchor your boat at the edge of the drop-off, outside of the heavy current. In some places you can fish from shore.

But there's one payoff spot I always look for when I fish below any dam: the slot. This is the noticeable line between fast-flowing downstream current and the eddy water that flows slowly back toward the dam. Bass lie below this, out of the current, dashing out to grab any passing food.

Try retrieving lures in the current outside the slot, using heavy tail-spinners (a minnow-body lure with a spinner at the tail end), jig-and-grubs, slab spoons, and deep-diving crankbaits. Also try using a casting bobber with a soft-grub jighead suspended below at varied depths. When a feeding spree ignites, you'll never forget the frenzy!

Weedbed margins

Now here is some of my favorite fishing. When you find marginal weeds bordering water from four to eight feet deep, you're in bass water. Keep the boat off a distance equal to your longest cast so you don't signal your presence to alert old bass.

Begin with surface lures such as slim minnows and tailspinners. Work them slowly and teasingly, as if they're ailing or dying, an easy meal. Try deep-diving plugs, first at the edge of the cover line, then keep working outward and deeper.

When you see a deep indentation, tie on an in-line spinner with a pork-frog trailer and cast it to the back edge. Work it out, first nudging the weeds, then working progressively deeper and at varied speeds.

Try weedless lures, such as plastic frogs or worms, that are cast into the weeds and powered through with lifts of the rod tip and intermittent reeling. Deep-running crankbaits in several sizes and colors are also practical here. As you keep moving, watch for movements of feeding bass. Stay as quiet as possible as you ease lures into the area, making your longest, most accurate cast.

Lily pad concentrations

These are natural sun shades that shelter bass from bright light, enabling them to see better with their fixed-aperture pupils. The bass lurk in the shadows, watching for dumb minnows to swim past in the sunlight. There are few places more exciting to fish than lily pads harboring big bass.

On calm days, try surface lures eased into open spots around the perimeters. Let them lie a long time before moving to give faraway bass time to come and eyeball the lures. When you move one, do it very gently, making the lure barely ripple the surface.

Giant 12-inch floating curlytail worms with no added weight, rigged weedless and cast far back into pad areas, are great. Make them swim all the way back, with the curlytail mussing up the surface. Use large 6/0 Kahle hooks on these for a big bite when you set the hook.

You can also try Texas-rigged plastic worms dropped into pockets. Let them sink to the bottom, yo-yo a couple of times, then slowly retrieve. Weedless spoons are good here, too. Use heavier lines, such as 20-pound test, for horsing big bass out of this tough cover.

Potent points

When you hear a bass fisherman say he was "point fishing" or "point hopping," he's referring to certain land fingers that form a point as they disappear into the water. There are many types of points, among them rocky ridges, the tip of an island, a steep bank coming to a point, or an elongated shoal, each end tapering off into the water. As bass cruise a lake, they stop and prowl around these areas to rest or to check on the food supply.

Some days the key to catching bass is to ply the points, and they can be potent. A good way to cover them effectively is to begin at the widest part of the point and work your way to the tip. Try a variety of surface and underwater lures cast directly into shore covers and worked from shallow to deep.

If that doesn't unlock their jaws, move in against the shore and cast out into deep water, using sinking lures such as jigs, plastic worms, spoons, and spinners. Let them sink to the bottom and fish them back deep. And finally, try working lures parallel to the shore at all depths.

Rocky shorelines

When I'm cruising a new lake, my eyes automatically lock onto rocky shores. I always try them because they pay off so consistently.

Ease in and check the size of the rocks and the angle of descent to get a feel for the nature of this area. If you're lucky, a nice breeze will be blowing parallel to shore. Let it waft you along as you cast obliquely ahead of the boat, which allows you to cover more area than casting directly ashore. Plastic worms are ideal for hitting shore hangouts and grubbing bottom on the way back.

Also try a variety of diving crankbaits with small to large lips, covering shallow to deep spots with these reliables. If the water is very clear, use natural colors. If it's dingy, use baits with rattles for extra sound attraction.

Big overhead spinnerbaits worked parallel with the bank do a good job of covering unseen lairs. Fish them slowly and deeply enough to feel them touching the rocky features. As a final shot before moving, put on a big-lip, extra-deep diver and troll the area—slowly at first; then try moving so fast the rod becomes hard to hold.

Shoals and reefs

These are various submerged formations, usually elongated, anywhere from a few feet deep on down to depths of 20 to 50 feet. It takes extra effort to locate those that aren't readily visible, but it's worth every hour.

One way to find them is to follow topographical maps and probe the depth contours listed. Another is to troll with a deep-diving lure; when your lure hangs on one of these features, pick out recognizable landmarks parallel with it, make a sketch of the location in your pocket notebook, which (of course!) you always carry with you. Then, if it proves to be a payoff spot, you can return to it again and again. Of course, a third and very reliable way is to invest in a sonar unit, which will quickly reveal these areas as you cruise a lake and watch the readings.

Shoals and reefs are potent bass hangouts because the bottom structure and vegetation provide habitation for all sorts of creatures in the bass's food chain. Fish topwater lures over shallow areas, work the deeper spots with bottom-touching lures, and fish both up and down the declines with a variety of deep-running lures. BIG bass can be had here!

Spring holes

These natural inlets of water are good bass hangouts all year. Up north their temperature is about 55°F year-round, while down south it stays about 70°F. This provides cool water during dog days when lake waters hit the 80s and warm water when winter water temperature drops into the 30s.

It's easy to locate spring holes flowing in from shore, and these should be fished year-round. To find those offshore takes some doing. A scuba-diving friend can locate them by water-temperature changes. My favorite tool is an electronic thermometer with a sensitive weighted probe that is lowered into the water until it touches bottom. As I slowly troll an area, it gives a constant temperature reading at three-second intervals. Once I locate a spot, I mark each spring with shoreline triangulations for future pinpointing. These holes will be good for ice fishing, too.

Several spring holes can be payoff spots when bass aren't in shoreline haunts. Vertical jigging with grubs, worms, or minnows pays off. Also, moving out about 30 feet and fishing plastic worms and crankbaits is effective.

THE TEN BEST STREAM HANGOUTS

When lakes settle into dog-day doldrums and bass are as scarce as two-dollar bills, it's time to fish moving water. Bass hangouts and feeding times are easier to determine in streams. There's just so much food in moving water: eels, leeches, crawfish, minnows, frogs, hellgrammites, salamanders, tadpoles, dragonflies, moths, snails, grasshoppers, and worms. Quite a "smorbassbord"!

I grew up bass fishing streams in southern Ohio and it's still in my blood, continuing to fascinate me. Unlike the repetitious shorelines of many lakes, streams offer variety and promise in every bend, cover, riffle, drop-off, pool, undercut bank, fallen tree, bridge buttress, eddy current and counterflow, culvert, inflowing creek, riprap, root cluster, gravel bar, island, boulder hole, bay, tailwater, and oxbow.

It's a different world than lake or reservoir fishing. Learning to read streams properly and catch bass requires new skills. I urge you to look over those streams in your area and make friends with them. For now, don your stream cap and let's go!

Proper gear

First, there's the boat. A low-cost craft, safe and maneuverable, is a 14- to 16-foot johnboat powered with a 25-horse outboard and a

Stream fishing, especially in fast currents, has its hazards—as in this one, which the guide didn't anticipate. Be careful not to drift into deadfalls; they can upset boats. Anchor outside of the current to fish this type of hole safely.

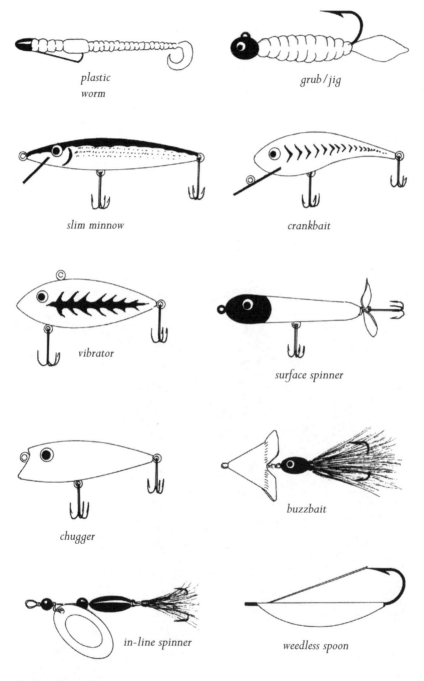

plastic
worm

grub/jig

slim minnow

crankbait

vibrator

surface spinner

chugger

buzzbait

in-line spinner

weedless spoon

Ten Best Stream Lures

minimum 35-pound-thrust electric. Equip it with fore-and-aft Danforth anchors, which will hold on sand, mud, or rocky bottoms.

Fishing rigs can be baitcasting, spincasting, spinning, or long poling, depending on your fancy. I suggest keeping your stream rigs on the light side, because stream bass average smaller and waters are much clearer. Take along at least three complete outfits suitable for casting lures of ¼, ⅜, and ½ ounce.

Lures should resemble the creatures that bass eat in shapes, colors, and sizes. You'll need sharp casting skills to ease them into bassy spots and animate them like the critters they're meant to represent. Here's a list of proven stream lures: plastic worms, jig-grubs, slim minnows, crankbaits, lipless crankbaits, surface spinners, chuggers, buzzbaits, in-line and over-head spinners, and weedless spoons. About three dozen assorted in natural colors and sizes (¼ to ⅝ ounce) will suffice for starters.

The hangouts

These are the ten top places bass dwell for two good reasons: they provide a spot for ambushing food and a place to rest between gorgings. Always approach these places stealthily, keep an easy-cast distance away, and handle oars and anchors as quietly as possible. Currents help carry your sounds to wary bass.

Riffles: Beach the boat and walk the shore above the deepest riffles. Position yourself at the head of the fastest water and cover every yard downstream, using these lures, which you can tote in a mini-tackle box: crankbait, spinner, jig-grub, plastic worm, lipless crankbait.

Pools: Anchor an easy cast from shore and work the dark drop-offs using plastic worms, crankbaits, lipless crankbaits, slim minnows, spinners, and buzzbaits.

Drop-offs: Work deep-diving crankbaits parallel to drop-off edges. Use slim minnows where the water is flat, and hop the bottom with spinners and jig-grubs.

Fallen trees: Coax plastic worms and weedless spoons through deadfall branches. Fish perimeters thoroughly with crankbaits, spinners, and jigs in the dark water around the main trunk.

Bridge buttresses: Anchor your boat parallel to the eddy water below the bridge support. In the flat water behind the buttress use slim

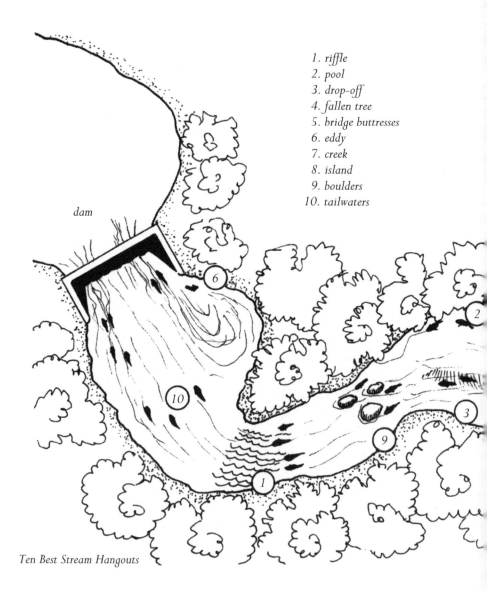

1. riffle
2. pool
3. drop-off
4. fallen tree
5. bridge buttresses
6. eddy
7. creek
8. island
9. boulders
10. tailwaters

dam

Ten Best Stream Hangouts

minnows and surface lures. In moving water use crankbaits, lipless crankbaits, plastic worms, and spinners.

Eddy currents: Below rapids or dam sluiceways, there's usually an eddy where the fast water rubs against the counterflow moving upstream. Fish this afoot from the head of the eddy, using jigs, plastic

worms, crankbaits, and spinners. In fact, try every lure in your kit in this hot hangout.

Inflowing creeks: These carry in nutrients for minnows to feed on and bring bass to chomp on the minnows. Use all the minnowlike lures in smaller sizes and natural colors.

73

Islands: These can hold a steady colony of bass. Fish the upstream edge using crankbaits, plastic worms, jig-grubs, spinners, and surface lures in quiet areas.

Boulder holes: Some boulders protrude above the surface; submerged boulders can be located by the slick water below them in fast currents. Cast sinking lures into the slick spots, especially plastic worms and jig-grubs.

Tailwaters: These are what fishermen call the flowing waters below a dam. They are a classic holding spot for bass because of the abundant food being washed over the dam. Find the nearest spot you can wade and make casts upstream into the deeper, slower-flowing water. Tie on a heavy casting bobber about two feet above a jig-grub lure, cast it upstream, and let the current bob the lure along. Try different depths by adjusting the bouncing bobber. I predict you'll be dam-well pleased with the bass and other species you catch!

9 The Three-Dozen Best Bass-Fishing Tricks

ven the best bass fishermen have days when they feel bass are finning their noses at them. Don't take it; fight back! Anyone can catch bass when they're bunched up on a feeding foray. But when they're scattered, finicky, full-bellied, and disinterested, remember these suggestions—three-dozen ways to turn a dismal day into a great one!

1. S-l-o-w d-o-w-n!

Frustrated anglers tend to fish faster, trying to cover more ground in an attempt to catch *any* bass. But wise elder anglers know it's time to slow down—*way* down, and fish each hangout with lures that do nothing, and do it very slowly. One way to ease yourself into the proper mood is to position your boat at the best angle to the target area using two anchors. Now saturate that spot with slow-moving lures of several types, and imagine that you have all week to fish.

2. Dawdle a floater

When the surface is flat, bass seem to turn up the volume on their sonar hearing aids; they're aware of anything that falls on the surface. Try casting a floating spinner lure or a slim minnow near cover and let it soak for at least a minute, watching it closely all the time. Then dawdle, twitch, coax, nudge, or urge it along about half an inch at a time. Imagine what's taking place out there in the bass's world. It becomes aware of shock waves from some critter barely moving on the surface.

As a predator, it's compelled to go see if it's an intruder or something to eat. Both are catching!

3. Soar a tube lure

These soft plastic tubes, about the size of your little finger with tendrils on the tail end, have earned a spot in every pro's tackle box as a result of their unique action. Rig one with a leadhead jig in the front of the tube and it spirals to the bottom. Rig it with the jig about halfway back and it soars slowly in a wide spiral. Before you fish one, go to a swimming pool and learn how jig placement affects the tube lure's action. Then go fish it!

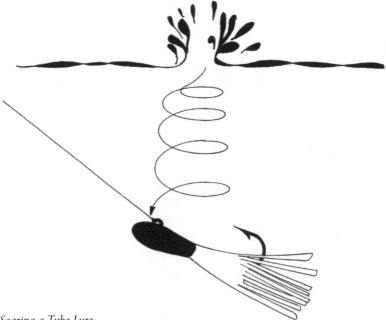

Soaring a Tube Lure
Adjust the leadhead jig inside the tube body—forward for a tight spiral, back for a wide pattern as it sinks.

4. Hump a spinner

Most overhead spinnerbaits come with average-size blades. For this maneuver, attach a big #6 blade to your favorite spinnerbait. Cast it out, and the instant it touches down, begin the retrieve. Reel just fast enough to make the spinner hump, but not break through, the surface. This brings big bass out of cover.

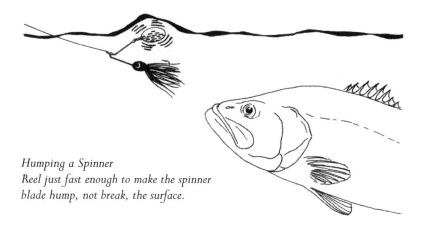

Humping a Spinner
Reel just fast enough to make the spinner
blade hump, not break, the surface.

5. Lighten up

Instead of a standard 6-inch plastic worm, scale down to a 3-inch worm. Instead of a slide sinker, just pinch a couple of split-shot onto the line about 6 inches above the worm. A 6-pound line will give it freedom of movement, and will be hard for the bass to see. Worked slowly over the bottom, it looks so helpless that bass charge in!

6. Flip your jig

To win a living from bass fishing, pros flip most of their lures, but only a few ordinary bass anglers know about flipping: It's the art of "pen-duluming" a lure softly into small targets. Done right, the reel spool never turns. The lure hangs suspended from the rod tip, even with the bottom of the rod. With an outward lift of the rod tip, the lure is softly eased into any pocket that might hold a bass. Practice at home, and once you master the skill, watch your bass catching double.

7. Hooked on hooks

That's Uncle Homer! Fine-quality hooks are an important part of bass catching. Ask your tackle dealer to show you hooks made by reputable craftsmen such as Eagle Claw, Mustad, Tru-Turn, or Gamakatsu.

These are sharpened to needle points, tempered to hold an edge. Regularly sharpen them on a honing stone; when the point hangs on your thumbnail, it's keen!

8. Scout 'em out

Turn poor bass days into good ones by taking the time to scout around, poking into areas other fishermen pass up, such as creek arms, backwaters, and old oxbow lakes. Keep notes about which is best, during both high and low water.

9. Helpful hope

Texas biologist John Hope studied five lakes over five years, tracking transistorized bass to establish patterns in their habits. One of his most helpful discoveries: Bass tend to layer at 8- to 12-foot depths in midlake waters, moving out each day to feed, then returning. So utilize this pattern by trolling open water at all depths to find them. A sonar is helpful to quickly pinpoint depths, drop-offs, ridges, and old streambeds—places where bass often congregate.

10. Instant weedless rig

Most bass fishermen like to fish the Carolina rig with exposed hooks, but these will hang on some bottom weeds. When this happens, use some wood toothpicks carried with you to push through the worm's body, just ahead of the hook. Break off the surplus pick and the worm will be weedless, but not fishless.

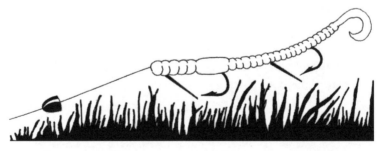

Instant Weedless Hook
A bare hook can be made instantly weedless by inserting a toothpick ahead of the hook point.

11. Watch water levels

When fishing reservoirs that were built to provide electric power, keep in mind that bass feeding times usually are tied to the up or down movement of the water level. Watch the banks as you fish to keep a constant check on this. Once you learn on which water movement the bass are feeding, you'll catch more fish.

12. Path to a giant

Although everyone dreams of catching that "biggest bass of their lives," most never really go for it. If you want that big bass, here are some things to remember: 1) Seek out the lake in your area that has produced the biggest bass over the years. Giantism is inherited; the fry of big bass are apt to grow into whoppers, too. 2) When you fish these select lakes, spend most of your time around known big-bass hangouts, such as cover edges bordering deeper, darker water; use larger lures than usual, like 12-inch plastic worms and 6-inch crankbaits with shiner color; fish more during dawn and dusk hours when big bass are on the feed. 3) Bigger bass like deeper water during midday hours. One of the best ways to reach them is to hook a 10-inch lively shiner in the lips and wind-troll it through the deepest holes.

13. Rattle a bass

Rattling lures are hot bass catchers, and a biologist with a hydrophone came up with a clue as to why. When schooling shad are dashing about, they make clicking noises with their jaws or gills. Bass hear this and come to investigate. Rattling lures may sound similar and bring bass. Whatever the attraction, rattlers are proven fish takers.

14. Hot-weather doldrums

Bass react to very hot weather about like we do: they're more active during the cool of the night. So join them by going after bass when most anglers are leaving the lake. If it's a calm night, use noisy surface lures fished slowly and rhythmically. It it's windy, use noisy underwater lures with rattles, sharply vibrating crankbaits, and spinner lures. An overhead spinnerbait gyrates as the lure falls. Let it spin its way to bottom, then retrieve it slowly and erratically with up-and-down movements of the rod tip. All appeal to the bass's sonar.

15. Trailer tactics

There's something magical about the addition of a trailer to spinnerbait, a wobbling spoon, or a leadhead jig. One theory is that the trailer sends out vibrations from the tail end, which is precisely what most aquatic creatures do with their caudal fins. Trailers are easy to come by: just attach a plastic worm, a piece of pork rind, or a curlytail grub—but be sure it's not so long that it takes away the flounce of a spoon. Activate the trailer with up-and-down nudges of the rod tip.

16. Think ahead

The best way to get maximum enjoyment from a day's fishing is to head off any foul-ups. Airplane pilots always use a checklist; here's a good one for bass fishermen: ice, food, drinks, first aid kit, sun and bug lotions, fishing rigs, tackle box, charged batteries; check electric and outboard motors for proper operation and boat and trailer for being properly secured; and advise someone where you'll be and when you'll be back. One final note before you launch the boat: Is the plug in?

17. Clarity disparity

What's the visibility range where you plan to fish? Here's a simple way to find out. Reel a bright yellow plug against your rod tip and push it vertically into the water. The distance at which it disappears is a good visibility gauge. A few inches means the water is dingy and calls for lures that vibrate, throb, rattle, or buzz to attract bass through their sonar sense. One- to 3-foot visibility calls for bright colors or flashy lures that bass can see more easily. Five feet and beyond is clear and calls for lures in natural, subdued colors, plus lighter lines so wiser old bass won't be wary of your offerings.

18. Savor the flavor

A surprising number of folks say they don't like fish because they smell and taste strong. The way to maximize eating enjoyment is to minimize the time from catching to cooking and to give fish proper handling between the two. A livewell with an efficient aerator will keep fish oxygenated and lively, but I prefer to place them in a plastic bag and store them in an ice chest. Clean the fish before leaving for home, keep the fillets cool, and wash and cook them as soon as possible. If you freeze fish, wrap fillets in plastic film, squeeze out all the air, place in a heavy-duty freezer bag, fill with water with no air space, and freeze quickly to avoid freezer burn. The average holding time for best flavor is one to six months.

19. Lining up properly

Always remember, the most important link between you and that whopper bass is your line. Before going fishing, always check your line for strength. Take three rigs: one with light line for clear water, one with medium strength for average water, and the third with heavier line for brushy areas. Take along spare line, and fish with confidence.

20. Plastic worming

As a rule, more than half the bass caught fall for the plastic worm. So fish worms more than half the time and keep these national statistics in mind. Best length—6 inches; best colors—purple, blue, black, red, brown, and motor oil; best rigging—Texas weedless with 3/0 single hook and ⅜-ounce slide sinker; preferred line—12-pound test; best tactic—cast rear cover, and as the worm settles to bottom, remember that this is when 75 percent of pickups occur. So have rod tip low, maintain light line tension to transmit feel, and the instant you sense any difference, set the hook with gusto. Hang on, and savor it!

21. Learn from pros

Only a choice few make a living as a pro bass fisherman, but I have fished with and studied the top twenty-five, so let me share their strategies. 1) Keep your mind thinking through the lure and learn to sense the difference in feel between touching cover and a bass pickup. 2) As you feel the lure along, keep scanning the water and select in advance the best likely hangout to lay the next cast. 3) Rig at least three rods with top-to-bottom lures and keep changing until a bass tells you which it prefers.

22. Trailer hook ploy

There are times when you feel fish nipping at your lure and wonder if it's bass or bluegills. This usually happens on single-hook lures such as spoons, jigs, or spinners with a pork-rind strip or soft plastic body. Try adding a trailer hook, 3/0 size, slipped over the single hook barb. To keep the trailer hook upright and centered on the main hook, add a bit of plastic worm above and below it. The next smart-alecky, short-biting bass will get the point!

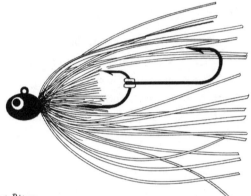

Cure for Short Biters
Attach a trailer hook onto a jig to catch "short biters." Small bits of plastic worm hold the trailer hook in line.

23. Portable piddler

Fishermen who drink lots of fluids need to eliminate them. We can't always go ashore or find a secluded spot on today's busy lakes. My solution is to carry a quart plastic bottle with a fist-size hole cut out just below the handle. On the jug is drawn a big, bold number 8. Inside one of the loops of the 8 are the letters *UR*. When a fishing buddy says he has to go, I hand him the jug and it begs the question: "What's the UR stand for?" And I reply, "Just what it says—'UR-in-eight.'" It's compact, easy to use discreetly, and you simply can't beat the price!

24. Unkinking line

Despite vigilance, tangled or twirling lures will twist line, making it virtually impossible to cast. Here are two effective ways to unkink twisted line: 1) Remove the lure and rapidly troll about half the line on your reel. Water friction will untwist it nicely. 2) If you're fishing from shore, tie a ball-bearing snap swivel to the end of the twisted line. Attach the snap to an unyielding tree limb, pay out about 25 yards of line, and walk away from the swivel until the line is taut. Jam your thumb against the line on the spool, then pull until you can feel the line stretching. This tension will cause the ball-bearing swivel to spin and remove all twist. It's a snap!

25. Shady strategy

When the sun's bright overhead, bass tend to head for the comfort of shade: under docks, piers, overhanging branches, duck blinds, and cutbanks. Seek out these spots, approach quietly, and offer these lures: surface-commotion types, floater-divers, deep-running crankbaits, plastic worms, jig-grubs, spinnerbaits, and weedless spoons. Don't hurry; the slower the better for coaxing out shaded bass.

26. Oldie/newie

Although buzzbaits have been around for a half century, they weren't really "on line" until the past ten years. Buzzbaits sound like a coot pattering over water as it takes off—you won't find a pro fisherman without a buzzbait. I urge you to spend several hours fishing only this weird lure to get the feel of casting and manipulating it around, through, and over all kinds of cover. It will catch bass when no other lure will. So put the buzz to 'em regularly.

27. Pier pressure

Piers are perfect hangouts for bigger bass. When one is caught out, another moves in. Here's how you should attack. First, try a plastic worm close to all sides of the pier. Next, hop a jig-and-pork rind over the

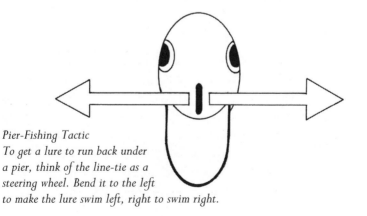

Pier-Fishing Tactic
To get a lure to run back under
a pier, think of the line-tie as a
steering wheel. Bend it to the left
to make the lure swim left, right to swim right.

bottom with minute twitches. Then try a big-lip crankbait that taps bottom. And finally, here's a finesse maneuver to reach big bass way under the pier. Say you're on the right side of a pier. Look a deep-diving plug square in the face and use a pair of long-nose pliers to bend the line-tie to the left. This will make the crankster run to the left, back under the pier, and nab bass that less ingenious fishermen miss.

28. Knock on wood

Woody things, such as brush, flooded timber, docks, piers, fences, pilings, and duck blinds, attract bass because they provide shade, food for little fish, and ambush points. After you've tried all your pet lures, try knocking on wood with these two. Try a big crankbait that floats lip down. The lip and body act like a bulldozer blade to guard the treble hooks from snagging on wood. Also try an in-line spinner with a big blade that shields the single hook from hanging up. Use both to knock against wood and bring bass from way off!

29. Spinner winners

Spinnerbaits are one of the all-time best bass catchers. Get out your pet spinnerbait, take off the spinner blade, and reattach it with a ball-bearing snap swivel. Buy these extra blades: French, willowleaf, Colorado, and Indiana, in sizes 2/0, 3/0, 4/0, and 5/0. Now when you go bass fishing you can quickly and easily change spinner blades. Use the big 5/0 for slow, shallow, and wobbly retrieves. Use the smaller blades for speedy, deep-running action. Usually, one of these blades is the magical cure for bass lockjaw. Keep changing until it happens!

30. Two-time 'em

Here's a ruse so old it's new to many bass fishermen: a tandem lure hookup. About 6 inches ahead of a crankbait, attach a swivel. From the front eye of the swivel, tie on a 6-inch length of 20-pound monofilament with a snap at the end. The snap will allow for easy changing of tandem lures and the stiffer dropper line will keep the lure from wrapping around the main line. Attach a large crankbait to the end of the main line, then try any of these on the dropper line: small spoons, streamer flies, curlytail jigs, tiny crankbaits, and 1/25-ounce in-line spinners. Big bass go for this rig because it looks like a predator (the large crankbait) stalking a tiny creature (the dropper lure). This makes the crankbait easy prey for the predacious bass.

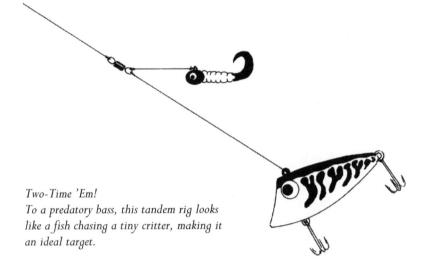

Two-Time 'Em!
To a predatory bass, this tandem rig looks like a fish chasing a tiny critter, making it an ideal target.

31. Match the catch

When you catch your first bass of the day and intend to eat it, take the time to examine its stomach content. You may find a crawfish, minnow, shad, bluegill, catfish, frog, or salamander. Gaze into your jam-packed tackle box and try those lures that closely resemble those critters in shape and color. Then activate the lure naturally. Matching is catching!

32. Play it cool

Did you know that temperatures in your tackle box can climb close to 200 degrees when it is sitting in the sun or confined in a car trunk? This is especially true if the tackle box is a dark, heat-absorbing color. This much heat will break down soft-plastic lures and even warp some hard-plastic models. The cure is to paint your tackle box a sun-reflecting color, such as white, yellow, or buff. And don't store your box in the trunk; it's better in the backseat with windows ajar for ventilation. When the heat's on, lighten up!

33. Drag check

A real reel problem is drag washers that lock up over night. The next day, when a whopper fish grabs your lure and takes off, the line breaks. Engineers are trying high-tech coatings and various lubricants, but have failed to solve this problem. The only safeguard is to set the drag adjustment at the beginning of each day's fishing, well below the line's breaking point. Don't forget!

34. Map preserver

Topo maps get dog-eared and soggy in a boat. Try encasing them in clear plastic sheeting available in office-equipment and wallpaper stores. Then roll the maps up for neat storage.

35. Direct descent

Big-lip crankbaits dive about 1 foot for each foot of retrieval. Let's say you're using a reel with a 6:1 retrieve ratio and a 3-inch spool diameter: this brings in about 18 inches of line with each turn of the reel handle. Thus in ten turns the big-lip lure should be about 15 feet deep—and about

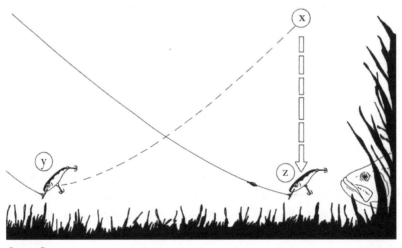

Direct Descent
When bass are secluded in heavy bottom cover, they won't pursue a lure that alights at X and takes course Y. But when a sinker is attached to the line, sinking the lure on course Z, right in front of the bass's nose, it's hard for the bass to resist such an easy meal.

the same distance from the cover holding the bass. So cast about 20 feet beyond the target area and reel steadily so the crankbait dives to the bottom; keep it coming, nudging the bottom cover. Hard to resist!

36. When you've lost it!

It happens to all veteran bass fishermen: You lose your touch, that sensitive feel that tells you when a bass inhales a tiny lure. Here's how to get it back. Rig a 12-foot graphite pole with an equal length of 4-pound line and tie on a ⅛-ounce curlytail jig. Take no other tackle with you. Move slowly and quietly around the shore cover in your favorite lake, easing the jig into nooks and crannies, then slowly yo-yo it up and down. By day's end your touch will be honed to a fine edge and you'll go home with a nice mess of panfish.

Seeing those spring lizards lolling on shore rocks in Dale Hollow Lake proved the key to a big-bass day. We baited and fished with brown plastic waterdogs, worked slowly and swimmingly, and Billy Burns (previous page) battled typical catch on this memorable occasion.

10 Uncle Homer's Ten Favorite Plastic Worm Wiles

There are many ways to fish the best-of-all bass lures, the plastic worm. But let me share with you Uncle Homer's top-ten tacks. They range from canny to crazy, but each can wangle your way to a bonanza day. Try each one for at least half an hour, then change. Use the ones that best fit the cover you're probing.

Let's begin with some preliminary observations to help set the stage before we tackle the top ten. First, worm colors. There are solid colors, bicolors, tricolors—the choices are endless. But a logical assortment would have to include the six best-selling colors across America. I've mentioned these before, but it's worth repeating: In order of usage, the best colors are only purple, blue, black, red, brown, and motor oil (also called punkinseed).

As for sizes, I suggest 4-inch, 6-inch, and 12-inch. Always begin with the popular 6-inch worm, and if the reaction is really blah, switch to the 4-inch size. When the whoppers are coming on, think BIG and offer them the 12-inch monster worm.

Hook sizes should conform to worm length: 2/0 for the four inch, 3/0 for the six, and 5/0 for the giant size. For slide sinkers, take along ⅛, ¼, ⅜, ½, and 1-ounce weights. Use a weight that casts well but makes the worm sink as slowly as possible. In really deep depths, use the 1-ounce to get down where they live. Now for the top-ten list.

1. Texas rig

This is the oldest, best, and most basic way to fish a plastic worm. You can cast it into a beaver's dam without snagging—usually. Cast it anywhere you think a bass might lurk and let it sink until slack line indicates it has bottomed. But "think sink." Keep your eye on the last foot of line above water and your mind on how the line feels throughout the sinking period. To feel a gentle bass pickup you must maintain a gentle tension on the line as the sinker pulls the worm downward.

Texas rig

About 75 percent of your pickups will happen now. Too much tension will pull the worm away from cover—and the bass. Most bass won't pursue the receding worm, so cast with a high rod tip and drop it fast when the worm hits the water.

No pickup? Hold it a sec; let's examine the mechanics of a pickup. As the worm settles, a watching bass can perform an amazing feat. By quickly opening its lower jaw and simultaneously flaring its gills, a bass can suck in a plastic worm from as far away as 15 inches. The worm literally *jumps* into the bass's maw, and it's this worm movement that you feel.

You have to picture that surge in your mind as you keep your eyes locked on the line. A sharp tug means the bass has sucked in the worm from the tail end, while a minute sideways move means a bass inhaled the worm from either side. A sudden "nothing" feel in the line means a bass has slurped the worm from above. When any of these occurs, reel slack out of the line as you lower the rod tip toward the bass, then set the hook with a fast two-hand movement of the rod tip from horizontal to vertical.

This hook-setting technique holds for whatever worm rig you're using. Just remember: It's speed in the rod tip that efficiently buries the barb, not a long muscular sweep.

2. Weightless worms

This is ultralight worming and calls for both ultralight rigging and a gentle hand. Use a spinning or spincast reel filled with 4-pound line and a soft-action rod. Tie on a 2/0 hook and rig a 6-inch, sinking plastic worm with no other weight. Waft this gently into all types of shore cover, slowly swimming a curlytail worm up, over, in, and around whatever obstacles it encounters.

weightless worm

Weightless worms work especially well when fishing duckweed or other surface weed masses. Cast far back and slowly inch the worm along to the outer edge of the mass. Here is where most strikes occur. Also, twitch the floating worm over the surface, close to all types of shore cover, especially in calm water.

3. Hi-vis Carolina rig

The purpose of a Carolina rig is to prevent the sinker from dragging a worm down into bottom cover where it's hidden from the bass's view. Some anglers attach a swivel about a foot above the hook, with a sinker above the swivel. I prefer to adapt my Texas rig to a Carolina quickly by toothpick-pegging the slide sinker to the line above the worm. This way it's easy to adjust for different worm elevations. Be sure the worm is a floater.

hi-vis Carolina rig

4. Monster worms

These foot-long whoppers have come through for me countless times. I use barely enough slip sinker to make the worm descend slowly and sinuously. When a bass inhales one of these, there's never a doubt about a pickup—the line literally spasms as that mass of plastic leaps into the bass's mouth. Retrieve it very slowly over bottom cover and crawl it with tail wiggling over and through shore covers. For surface fishing, no sinker is needed; the worm alone is heavy enough.

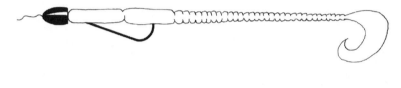

monster worm

5. Midget worms

When the water is extremely clear and bigger bass are hard to entice, go for the kid bass, 1- to 2-pounders. Use ultralight rigs and barely enough weight to sink a 4-inch worm on a 4-pound line. Make longer casts than usual, using subdued colors such as motor oil, and work the worm much slower than usual.

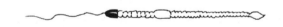

midget worm

6. Twirl-a-rig

This tactic gives wise old bass an action they've probably never seen, unless I've been to your good hole. Rig a slide sinker on your line, then tie on a ball-bearing snap swivel. Next add a 3/0 hook to the snap, and rig a plastic worm so that it has a hump in its back. This will twirl without twisting line and entice big bass.

twirl-a-rig

Cast this rig into all types of shore cover such as lily pads, weed patches, cattails, brush, standing timber, etc., and reel just fast enough to cause the worm to gyrate. Try different shapes of humps for variety. A faster spin seems to work best in clear water, slower when it's murky.

This rig can be very productive for deepwater bass fishing, say 20 to 30 feet down, and also in riffles where streams enter a lake or flow into a deep hole. Here's one more situation; try trolling v-e-r-y slowly just outside dense shore cover abutting deep water.

7. Twin worms

I learned this ploy from a native guide in Honduras, and it's worth trying from time to time. Tie on two hooks instead of one to the end of your line. Texas-rig a 6-inch plastic worm on each, and make the colors very contrasty, such as bright yellow paired with stark white.

This could be called a twin-Texas rig, because you have two weedless worms working for you instead of one. This gives twice the vibration to attract bass in murky water, and in clear water it can entice bigger bass by offering two worms in one gulp. Keep changing colors until you hit the right combination.

Now let's take this twin-worm one step further. Tie on two 5/0 hooks, using at least 20-pound test line. Then add two giant 12-inch plastic worms with big curlytails, and be sure they are floaters, rigged weedless. Cast these to the back of surface cover like lily pads, floating

twin worms

weeds, and brushy areas. Crawl the whopper worms over the surface and you will be amazed at how faraway bass will come to attack.

You can also add enough slide sinker to the line to sink this pair of behemoth worms, and fish them outside shore cover where it drops off into dark water. Inch them over the bottom, and when a big bass latches on, you'll be thankful for that 20-pound line!

8. Jiggly worm

I know it sounds silly, but don't laugh until you try it; a lot of experts are catching bass on it. First the rigging: Using a 3/0 hook, impale a 6-inch plastic worm crosswise through the thick segment of the body. Both ends will droop down. Cut off a roofing nail until it measures about 1 inch, including the flat head. Insert the nail into the worm's head until it's buried to the nailhead.

Here are two very good ways to fish it, using an ultralight outfit.

• Cast the jiggly worm into cover pockets and let it slowly settle to the bottom. You'll get most of your pickups as it sinks; there's something very tempting about this poky descent versus the plunging drop of a slip-sinker rig. If you don't get a strike, raise your rod and as you slowly retrieve line, constantly shake your rod tip. This causes the jiggly worm to make minute spasmodic twitches.

• For what may be your biggest catch of the day, try this in deep water around bridge abutments, over old roadbeds, alongside docks, and in flooded timber. Quietly anchor your boat right against these. Have a cold drink to slow your reflexes and give the bass a chance to forget you're there.

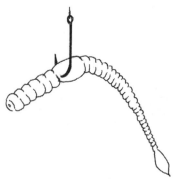

jiggly worm

Let the jiggly worm settle to the bottom, directly below you, until the line goes slack. Raise your rod tip about 6 inches and begin yo-yoing the worm up and down, using very gentle lifts and dips of the rod tip. This makes the middle-hooked worm ends appear to be gently finning it around. Keep doing this until the line suddenly feels different, indicating that a bass has gently sucked in this jiggler. Set the hook. And remember, I told you so!

9. Chambered worm

These might be a little hard to find where you live, but keep looking. Chambered worms have a pocket molded into the body that can be used to make these worms perform stunts impossible with regular worms. One type has a pouch in the middle section where you can insert a piece of foam for extra buoyancy in surface fishing or when using it in a Carolina rig. Or you can insert a gob of scent, now available in many forms.

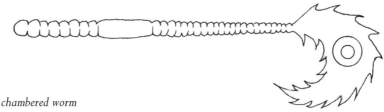

chambered worm

Another chambered worm comes with a pocket in an oversize curlytail section that emits sharp vibrations. These worms come in a kit with several plastic balls containing tiny metal shot. Insert a rattling ball into the tail pocket and the curlytail sounds off as it flutters. You can also add scent for extra attraction.

Some anglers have gone so far as to stuff live worm bits into these pockets to give out a natural smell and taste. And if you're fishing in very deep water, you can add split shot to the chamber to sink these pocketed worms.

10. Innard weighting

Take along a coil of wire solder, the largest diameter you can find. Cut off two-inch lengths of it and insert just enough into the worm body so that it barely sinks. Cast close to cover, and try to be patient until slack in the line tells you the worm has reached bottom. Then s-l-o-w-l-y work it over the bottom, all the way back. This is especially effective in very clear water.

That ends Uncle Homer's top-ten worming tricks, any one of which could turn an off day into an on day, and turn you into a thinking bass catcher!

11 The Six Catchingest Live Baits

In the beginning there were fish in the water, and man and worm on land. It was inevitable that the three should get together. Man could no more resist fashioning a hook to catch those fish than he could resist finding a female and caving up. Ever since, it's been tough to determine who has been more hooked: fish, worm, or man. We do know this: Many a garden goes to pot because the first spadeful of earth uncorks a bunch of wiggling worms.

So when you hear a sporty fisherman mouth off about a "worm dunker" or "live bait sort" as bad for the sport, pity his ignorance. If the live-bait fisherman hadn't needed sensitive tackle to present his offerings more stealthily and skillfully, there would have been no money to build the factories that produce the sophisticated tackle that the sporty angler uses. Live-bait fishing is just as much a skilled art as fishing artificial lures. But there is more to the skills than meets the casual eye.

America's six most popular live baits are worms, minnows, crawfish, waterdogs (salamanders), frogs, and hellgrammites. But just because a fisherman dangles them in front of a bass doesn't guarantee that the bass will eat them. Like humans, bass can be choosy feeders, so the selection and presentation of these creatures are important. Let's study these six great baits in the order of their national popularity, from the most to the least.

1. Worms

Worms range from the wriggly red garden variety to large, slinky nightcrawlers. I prefer the biggest worms for the biggest bass.

Nightcrawlers are so called because they come out at night to make love in the grass. By sneaking up on them with a flashlight and making a quick grab, you can nab two at once—unless you happen to be a romantic.

Rig them as illustrated here and present them quietly and close to any of the bass hangouts previously described. You can do this with or without a bobber; try them both ways. When a bass sucks in the worm, wait a few seconds, then set the hook. Enjoy: It can add years to your life.

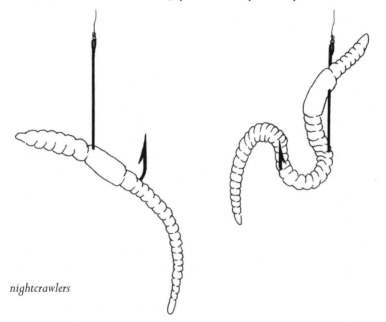

nightcrawlers

2. Minnows

Minnows come in many sizes and species; to a fisherman, any small fish is a minnow. Technically, a minnow is a member of the carp family, but bass aren't finicky about ancestry. If it looks like a fish, they eat it! However, certain species do seem to produce more bass, and these are shad and shiners, found in most lakes and live-bait stores. Choose lively ones, and have a good aerator to keep them lively. A little ice to keep waters cool also helps.

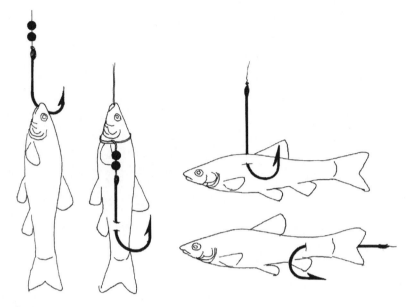

minnows

Use a sturdy rod with line to match—40-pound-test—so you can wrestle whopper bass out of heavy cover. Hook an awesome minnow, like a 10-incher, through the tail, and keep pitching it close to heavy shore cover until it runs way back under.

Don't expect many explosive strikes. When a big bass inhales a minnow, you feel a series of gentle tugs. The bass has the minnow inside its huge mouth and is both crushing and scaling it. If it has taken the minnow tail first, the bass first must blow the bait out in order to take it head first to avoid its spiny dorsal fin. Wait until you feel a steady pull on your line, then set the hook, keep a tight line, and enjoy what you came for!

3. Crawfish

Crawfish are to bass what aged fried ham is to country boys. But first you have to get the crawfish. You can do this either with a seine in a stream or with a few bucks in a live-bait store.

As all crawfish anglers know, the choicest is a "softshell." When a crawfish outgrows its shell, it splits it open down the back, crawls out, and hides from predators until its soft new shell hardens.

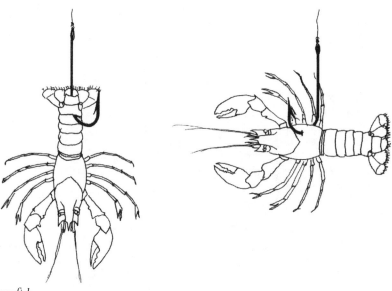

crawfish

Softshells are hard to come by, but I'll share with you a little secret that some of the tight-mouthed crawfisherman in your area would rather you didn't know. As mentioned, growing larger splits a crawfish's shell. Seine for them below a slaughterhouse or a food-processing plant that dumps nutrients into a stream, and you can catch a steady supply. Nowhere do they eat, split, and get soft more often than here.

Hook crawfish as shown here, and retrieve them slowly over the bottom in bass hangouts. The tail hookup is for casting; it lets you work the crawfish backward, just as it usually moves. The body hookup is for fishing with a bobber or dunking with a long cane or graphite pole. This is one super bass bait!

4. Waterdogs

These live everywhere except in big cities and are known by other names such as salamanders, newts, efts, chameleons, and lizards. They have soft, scaleless bodies and would crowd a lively minnow for top honors in catching big bass.

Where we live in suburban Florida, dozens hang around in our garage, yard, and porches. They are bug eaters, have little fear of man, and are easily caught if you just sneak up on them with a net. Most bait

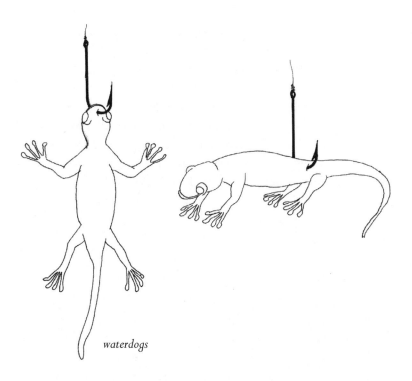

waterdogs

houses sell them. If you want to catch your own, stalk them in marshes, around cool springs, and in streamside brush.

When fishing a waterdog, remember this oddity, which explains why they make such an effective big-bass bait. Waterdogs are egg eaters, so bass hate them as a mortal enemy. As soon as they see one they'll attack it, kill it, then blow it out. When you feel a take, you'll have only a few seconds before the bass ejects its enemy, so set the hook hard with a strong line.

Fish waterdogs around all types of cover: over bottom, around trees, off deep shorelines, and in backwaters. Keep moving and fishing until you get a strike so vicious it knocks off your fishing hat. Then you'll know why I like waterdogs!

5. Frogs

These homely croakers have long, lithe legs for leaping and swim-ming—and to keep one jump ahead of the numerous predators that feed on them, including bass.

The handiest tool for capturing frogs is a long-handled net. And when you go frogging, it's smart to take along a youngster with very fast reflexes, unless, of course, you are so blessed. Frogs are out during all warm months, near water edges.

As you grasp a frog and it looks you in the eyes, you can't be sensitive if you're to be a worthy frog fisherman. Ignore the way those soft bug-eyes bore into you. Pay no heed to the almost human way it imploringly clasps your fingers with its three-toed hands. Go ahead and shove that hook where it belongs, softheartedness be damned.

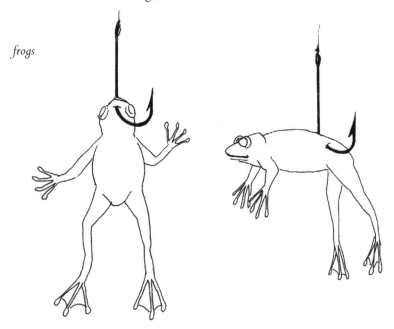

frogs

Flip that frog into lily pad pockets, near weed margins, and drift it into deep holes. When a big bass gulps down that frog, give it time to exert a strong pull on the line, then set the hook. From the moment you heft your whopper bass, you'll become a die-hard frog impaler. And you'll sleep well!

6. Hellgrammites

If you're a stream fisherman, here is a choice bass bait only the insiders know how to catch and fish. A hellgrammite, the larval stage of the dobson fly, is very ugly, but it must look mighty pretty to a bass, judging by the way they slurp them in.

Catching hellgrammites is a two-man job. One gets on the downstream side of rocks in a swift section of stream and holds a net. The upstream man turns over rocks, to which the hellgrammites cling, and they wash into the net.

Stick a long-shank hook into the hellgrammite's tough, segmented body, as shown, and drift it into deep holes or dunk it near bass hangouts. If it insists on grabbing weedy cover and hanging on, snip off the twin pinchers on its tail end.

Also try a casting bobber in slow, deep flows. Add one split-shot 6 inches above the bait and keep raising the bobber until the hellgrammite just nudges bottom. Keep making these probing drifts until the cork heads for the bottom.

If bass are still reluctant, maybe they have full bellies. Try pulling off the hellgrammite's head and collar and turn it inside out. If this doesn't do it, it's a hellgrammite of a note and time to try something else.

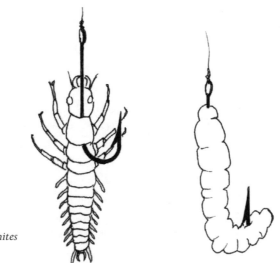

hellgrammites

12 The ABZs of Surface Fishing

Uncle Homer is about to lay on you the basic knowledge needed to catch bass on top—wily ways to make big bass "come up like thunder" to murder surface lures, plus offbeat tactics that goad bass into striking when they hadn't the slightest intention of doing so.

But before we get our heads together, let's have an understanding: Surface fishing is no easy game. It's far more exacting than fishing plastic worms and even more demanding than fly fishing. Selling a canny bass on a boisterous topwater lure is akin to selling a concert lover on the cultural values of a calliope. It's got to be very good!

And *you've* got to be very good to sell wise elder bass on things that chug, splutter, burp, gurgle, hiss, and spit and do any number of antics that make them look utterly unlike things bass normally eat. But this is the art of surface angling. You don't appeal to your quarry's appetite so much as its weakness for being duped—much like a carnival pitchman and a country boy.

To become a master surface fisherman you almost need to grow a pair of gills, an underslung jaw, and a pair of bulging, critical eyes so that you can comprehend a bass's views on what you do with topwater lures.

As a matter of fact, there isn't one topflight surface fisherman who couldn't improve his skills by lying on the bottom of a swimming pool in a scuba outfit, looking up at surface lures being manipulated over his head. He'd immediately notice two things: how little movement is required to muss up the surface and emit shock waves that bounce off both sides of the pool, and how very audible, even to his ears, these minute movements are.

If you aren't a scuba fan, try the same thing, only holding your breath for a half minute at a time. By briefly inserting ourselves into the world of the bass, we get a much better sense of what's happening at the end of the line.

Even as I begin, I know I'll be guilty of two faults. One is not listing more native ways to surface-fish; the other is listing some that are as obvious as a gorilla in a church choir. Amen!

So I'll make you a deal: I'll appreciate it when all you "natives" tell me about your odd ways I didn't cover. And I'll appreciate your patience as I list some basic fundamentals that are of interest mostly to surface-fishing neophytes.

PROPER TACKLE

Surface fishing requires heavier tackle than needed in open water. You're going to be catching bass, *big* bass, around many kinds of cover where they can become entangled. This calls for a versatile fishing rig with muscle.

I prefer two rods of different lengths. One is a 7-footer with a 10- to 12-inch-long butt section on the handle. The 7-foot length gives me leverage for long casts into wayback pockets. It also helps me lever up a big bass's head and muscle it out of trouble.

My second rod is a 5- or 6-footer to make short, accurate casts. With it I can impart more minute animations to sensitive lures than I can with a longer rod. Both rods must have tips that respond to lures from ¼ ounce upward and butts with enough muscle to keep a lunker bass from bashing its way into heavy cover. Most of the time a 20-pound-test line is adequate for these needs.

The reel, be it casting, spincasting, or spinning, must function smoothly, with quiet ball-bearing friction points and precision gearing, to take the punishment that surface fishing demands. Buy the best quality you can afford.

COVER IS KEY

A good topwater fisherman must learn to read bass cover like a road map. Once you get the knack, your eyes will constantly search for any spot where a bass might be hiding. You also learn to recognize some of the unlikely spots other anglers pass up, especially those they deem too tough to reach. *You* don't, though, because you've learned how. Practice, practice!

Typical places include pockets or insets in lily pads or weedbeds; rifts running through weedy clusters; alongside fallen logs or trees; behind off-shore weed fringes; around stumps; beneath piers, docks, or duck blinds; beside abutments; under overhanging brush or banks; over reefs or shoals; in eddy water; around cattail clumps. In short, look for any cover that will provide shade and concealment. And don't forget to probe places too tough, too far, or unlikely for the casual bass fishermen to attempt.

LEARN THE TECHNIQUE

Watch a master surface-lure angler and you'll see someone who has spent years honing his skills. Surface fishing is an art that calls for casting lures accurately into small hangouts, and you can learn this at home. Just practice until you can drop a ⅜-ounce hookless plug onto a garbage can lid three out of five casts at about 40 feet.

The instant your lure touches down, the real challenge begins: manipulation. Imagine yourself as a magician holding a magic wand—your fishing rod. Every movement of your rod tip breathes life into that distant lure. Your audience members are bass, and your challenge is to make them think that lure should be driven away or gulped down.

The artistry lies in coordinating the timing between rod-tip twitches and reeling slack out of the line to keep it taut. The lure responds according to its design and the spacing of your twitches. It's a skill you acquire only through watching accomplished surface-lure fishermen and deciding which of their touches to add to your bag of tricks. That, plus honing your hand-, eye-, and lure-manipulation skills through hours of effort until it becomes instinctive.

LET'S TALK LURES

To simplify what can be a very confusing conglomeration of lures, let's separate them into generic types: floater-spinners, sinker-spinners, poppers, slim minnows, wobblers, buzzbaits, dog-walkers, bloompers, stickbaits, and soft naturals. Each type has a personality all its own.

Here are ways of fishing these lures that I've found productive in more than a half century of fishing on four continents. Try them, but add your own personal magic. In addition to basic tactics for each type of lure, I've also added what I call thunder tactics. These are trickeries that go one step beyond the usual to trigger reflexive strikes from bass, even when their bellies are full.

Floater-spinners

These lures float at rest and have one or two spinners, usually of the propeller type. When pulled forward, the water twirls the propellers, causing them to sputter. The resulting commotion attracts bass for two reasons: the noise is much like a bass slashing into minnows, causing other bass to come join the feeding; and the lure resembles a struggling creature that could make an easy meal.

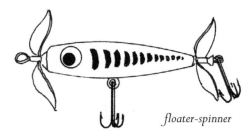

floater-spinner

Basic tactics

There are endless ways to work a lure of this type, but here are some steady bass catchers. Any could be the key to catching bass at a particular time of any day. Cast the lure very close to cover. Let it lie for five to ten seconds, then twitch it ever so lightly, just barely enough to cause the spinner blades to turn over. Repeat the maneuver all the way back to your rod tip.

Another method is to start the lure in motion the instant it touches down, keep it twitching and sputtering in terse spurts, like a frightened creature heading for cover. Also try a slow, steady retrieve with no pauses.

Thunder tactic

Very clear water can pose a problem. When a bass moves in close for a critical look and hesitates, you'll need to goad it into striking by appealing to its reflexive instincts. Choose the lightest color and smallest lure you have, and no matter which basic tactic you use, keep the lure in continuous, turbulent motion. The strategy is not to let the bass ever see the lure clearly. As you hurry it along, keep your rod tip low, ready to strike when Ol' Bigg'n blasts the bejazus out of it.

In tannic or roily water, where visibility is limited and a bass must get very close to get a good look at a lure, here's a thunder tactic meant to amplify the spinner sound many times. Take the spinner off your lure and lay it on a metal coffee-can lid. Make an outline twice the size of the spinner and cut it out with tin snips. Bend the blades into the same profile as the original spinner and drill a hole in the center. Attach this monster to your lure and retrieve in short, quirky jerks. When its vibratory message reaches a bass's sonar, it says: "I'm big enough to fill a *big* belly!" Only *big* bass will respond.

Sinker-spinners

This family of lures is made up of several types, none of which resembles bass food, yet they are among the top six all-time bass catchers. Let's examine the best designs. The most popular is an overhead spinner, or spinnerbait, with a body shaped like an open safety pin. To the overhead arm is attached a spinner blade, and below this is a body, usually skirted, resembling a minnow. The next most popular is an in-line spinner, with a spinner blade and body, usually skirted, on a single shaft.

spinnerbait

Basic tactic

If you begin your retrieve the instant the lure touches down, an overhead spinnerbait becomes a very different looking surface lure. An in-line spinner can also be worked on top at a fairly slow retrieve. To achieve superior surface commotion, oil the spinner-blade attachment of either type to ensure it's working freely. Fish the lure in and around dense-cover shore hangouts, keeping it coming on or barely under the surface for the noisiest spinner commotion.

Thunder tactic

The added resistance of an extra-large spinner blade—say a size 6 or 8 willowleaf—on an overhead spinnerbait makes it easier to keep it on or barely under the surface. To make changing blades easy, replace the split-ring holding the spinner blade with a ball-bearing snap swivel. Keep changing blades until you find the one that best balances that particular lure. You'll be pleased at how easy it is to work a spinnerbait as a surface lure.

You can replace the blade of an in-line spinner with an oversized French blade for the same effect. Add a pork-rind trailer for buoyancy, and retrieve at both slow and fast paces, over and barely under the surface.

When a bass takes either of these spinners, give it slack line for a count of three, then set the hook *hard*—and once again for good measure.

Poppers

These noisy lures are easily recognized by their hollow or cupped heads. When jerked, they make a popping sound; hence the name. They come in all sizes from tiny to magnum, and most have two treble hooks. Some are weedless with single or double hooks. At times, no lure can match them.

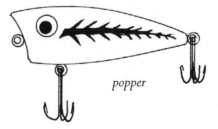

popper

Basic tactic

Just cast near cover and pop it. Try to make it stay in one spot a long time. See how many different movements you can impart with your rod tip. It's amazing how one particular quirk can bring beautiful bashes.

Also try various sizes, from small to large, in order to get a full range of popping sounds. Note how a gentle twitch can make a popper spit little sprays of water, a sharper twitch will make an audible pop, and a violent jerk a loud *whoooomp*! Keep trying them all.

When you find the right-size popper and the magical sound that turns bass on in a certain lake, stay with it. It's surprising how any one of these can be the key on one lake but not on others. No one knows why, it just is. Some studious topwater specialists keep notes on key lures and tactics, in addition to best times of year.

Thunder tactic

You won't believe this one until you try it. When it works, I don't know any trick that makes a fellow feel more like Merlin the magician. You'll have to add a big machete to your "might-come-in-handy" tools; a rake will do.

When bass aren't responding to your best offerings, especially during dog-day doldrums, they're usually in deep seclusion in the heaviest covers. Look for heavily matted weed areas where the water is 3 to 5 feet deep. Ram your boat into this mass and use your tool to clean out a 6- to 8-foot hole. As you depart, carve out a slot leading to open water.

Leave for an hour or more to give bass time to forget you were there. Their minds will be on minnows, which came to dine on plankters released by your cuttings. Anchor a long-cast distant and drop a small popper in the center of the hole.

Let it lie motionless for a ten-count, then just make it spit with a gentle twitch.

Now begin your full range of trickery. If none of your efforts does the job, then stand up and jerk the popper until it *swoosh*es, and keep it coming. This can be like dynamite!

Slim minnows

These long, slim, minnow-shaped lures with the quick, enticing wiggle weren't really designed as surface lures; they have a lip to make them dive on the retrieve. Yet since their introduction they have proven to be one of the all-time best surface lures.

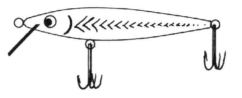

slim minnow

Basic tactic

These lures are a beginner's delight. Just cast one near cover, twitch it a few times, and retrieve just fast enough to make it dive under. Also try making it dart occasionally with twitches or any other animation you think looks enticing. This is one lure it's hard to fish wrong; just stay with it.

Thunder tactic

Tie a snap swivel about a foot in front of the slim minnow on a 3-inch dropper line. Impale on the snap a 2-inch white curlytail grub. When moved, the grub's curlytail gives off lifelike flutters. Cast close to cover and let it lie for a moment to get a nearby bass's attention. Then give the lure a sharp twitch. This causes the slim minnow to dart and the grub to wiggle as if trying to ecape. What a target for a husky bass!

Wobblers

These unusual lures were designed to wobble with a noisy action when reeled steadily. The resulting turbulence could resemble a mouse, frog, waterdog, even a baby muskrat scurrying over the surface. Wobblers are ideal for beginners, but I still get a kick out of working them because of their versatility. Two longtime performers that have been catching bass for three generations are the Jitterbug and the Crazy Crawler. Retrieved

Jitterbug   *Crazy Crawler*

at a steady pace, they waddle seductively. Or they can be popped, chugged, danced, or wobbled in a variety of ways.

Basic tactic

No doubt this is the simplest surface lure to call on. Just cast it near shore covers and reel it steadily while it does its thing. Bass sometimes bird-dog the commotion and bash it right next to the boat. Normally a steady pace is best. At times a stop-and-go retrieve is effective, like an injured, aged, or dying critter trying to make it ashore. As you use these, you will come up with your own variations. Try the smaller sizes in spring, when offspring of many types hatch out and look like an easy meal.

Thunder tactic

This ploy takes some teamwork but it's worth the time, especially when the water is very calm. Cast a wobbler near shoreline cover and let it lie motionless for a few seconds. Your partner then casts a slim-minnow floater about 2 feet behind the wobbler. The moment his lure lands, start wobbling your lure toward you. He then keeps his swimming minnow coming about a foot behind your wobbler, as if stalking it and making occasional darts at it.

Most of the time a bass will clobber the stalker, thinking it's easy prey. Other times bass try to beat the stalker to the stalkee and bash the wobbler. It's like holding a two-for-one sale—and it's not unusual to get two customers at once.

Buzzbaits

These lures have been around since the early 1930s, but they finally hit a popularity peak about a decade ago and are still going strong. Curiously, a buzzbait is a surface lure that sinks at rest yet is worked on

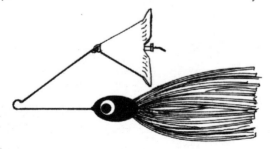

buzzbait

top. The double or triple blade is an exaggerated propeller that causes the lure to rise to the surface when lifted and retrieved. It makes a loud, spluttering sound and churns the surface into a trail of bubbles.

Some buzzbaits are made of a buoyant plastic; others have built-in squealers or rattlers. How old are buzzer-type baits? Well, Julio Buel was granted a patent for the first American spinner lure about 1850. And local fishermen used them on a cane pole with a short line, making a noisy "figure eight" for bass—and this buzz caught a lot of monsters.

Basic tactic

Most of the time you need only cast out and keep the spinners churning over the surface with their "I-dare-you" splutters, the sound waves of which bring big bass out of heavy cover or up off the bottom. Buzz them over, around, through, and just touching all kinds of cover. Buzzbaits will grow on you once you gain confidence in their effectiveness.

Thunder tactic

It's rare that you need to call on a thunder tactic with a buzzbait. But here's one to try when you're desperate. Cast close to the edge of heavy cover, buzz the lure several feet, then let it sink out of sight. Reel it to the surface, buzz several feet, and let it sink. This rise and fall is erratically enticing!

Dog-walkers

I use this name because it's what devotees call the unusual antics it performs when coaxed into action by a skilled angler. Dog-walkers make more commotion and require more hand—eye timing than all other surface lures. A dog-walker is shaped like a fat cigar, about 5 inches long, and floats at about a 20-degree angle, tail down, with the head protruding above the surface. It has no built-in action and lies stone dead—until an expert animates it.

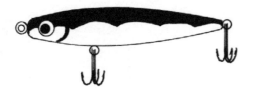

dog-walker

Basic tactic

When the surface is calm, cast near cover and let the lure lie while you slowly reel slack out of the line. Gently twitch the lure until it turns sideways. With a short twitch of the rod tip, the head of the lure will swing to the opposite side. Quickly reel in slack and give the lure a terse twitch to swing the head to the other side. Once you master the rhythm and timing, keep it coming, darting from side to side, unlike anything most bass have seen.

This is called "walkin' the dog," which, in your grandma's day, meant sashayin' from side to side and puttin' on a show—an apt description of the action fishermen exact from this lure.

Thunder tactic

This one may surprise even veteran dog-walkers, who normally think of using this lure type only on calm water in order to get maximum commotion. Let's say there's a sizable chop on the surface and the bass are doing nothing. Put on a dog-walker and begin working it near shoreline covers. When I say work it, I mean stand up, make a long cast, and with the rod tip low do some energetic twitching that makes that dog-walker slap the water hard, throwing up splashes. This has saved many hopeless days for ol' Unc.

Bloompers

On this peculiar breed of surface plugs, the faces aren't hollow like poppers but are of a different cut, such as semicircular or with a flat, crosswise angle. The sounds they make are on the soft side, more *bloomps* than pops, hence the odd name. Poppers have no built-in swimming action, but bloompers have this as an added attraction. The best-known lures of this type are Heddon's Lucky 13 and South Bend's Bass-Oreno.

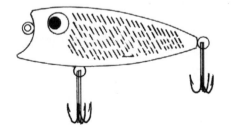

bloompers

Basic tactic

Cast near cover, let it lie, then twitch just enough to bring out the lure's slurping sound. Slurp it a couple times, twitch twitch, *bloomp bloomp,* then s-l-o-w-l-y reel it in, and be ready for strikes anywhere in between.

Thunder tactic

Add a small plastic worm or a strip of pork rind to the tail hook. Make it a prominent color like yellow or white. Cast near cover and go through your usual routine of twitches, but wait longer than usual between casts. As the bloomper lies there, the trailer is in constant motion and adds a subtle attraction to the lure.

Stickbaits

The quietest of all hard surface lures and one of the least-often used, the stickbait has no features that produce sound, and therein lies its effectiveness. At times, bass simply want a quiet lure, and only the bass know why. All stickbaits share a basic design feature: They are very slim and long, tapering at both ends, and at rest they float vertically with nothing but the tip of the nose above water.

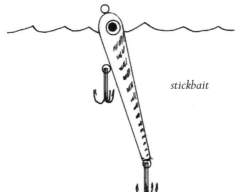

stickbait

Basic tactic

Cast near or over bassy cover, and let the stickbait lie still for at least a slow ten-count. Then, hold your breath while you gently twitch your rod tip—barely enough to make the stickbait nod its head. Note that I said nod, not thrash. Keep in mind, this lure is the quiet one.

Thunder tactic

This trick works best in clear water when bass are shying away from more boisterous surface lures. You're going to make the stickbait nod, like making a curt "Howdy," but you're going to do it about once each second. Keep nodding and reeling so that the stickbait's head dimples the water every couple of inches, all the way back. It's tricky to do but worth the effort, because how many bass have seen a lure do this?

Soft Naturals

These soft plastic lures look and feel like some of Mother Nature's finest swimming over the surface. Over the years we've seen these in birds, dragonflies, moles, chipmunks, rats, and snakes. But the enduring ones are frogs, mice, and eels. Most are weedless, rigged with widespread double hooks that fit into body contours so they can be retrieved in dense cover.

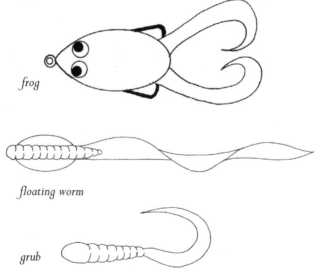

frog

floating worm

grub

Basic tactic

Cast a mouse or a frog into all kinds of snaggy hangouts, like brush, weeds, lily pads, and cattails. Keep in mind how each might move over water, and duplicate the action with your frog or mouse. Swim the 12-inch eel slowly and invitingly along.

Thunder tactic

Give the mouse a tail. This is easily done by attaching a 4-inch plastic worm to the rear end, using a trailer hook if necessary. When reeled or twitched it gives extra movement and appeal.

And try this with the frog: Look for a large lily pad lying in dark water and see how sharp a caster you really are by plopping the frog onto the pad leaf. Let it lie, then move it only a fraction of an inch at a time. A nearby bass will feel these vibes and watch it like a hawk. When you finally twitch it off the pad, have your rod tip low and be ready to set the hook, hard!

Now to the giant worm's thunder rig. This is going to challenge your ingenuity. The 12-inch worm is a high floater, but add barely enough split shot to the line just ahead of the hook to sink only the head of the worm. Twitch this along over a flat surface in shallow water. The sunken worm head looks like a snake searching for food while the wiggling tail propels it along.

That covers surface lures. Remember, fishing them is both an art and a learned skill, and thinking through them is a discipline. But the rewards are worth the effort!

13 What Sounds Make Bass Bite?

Human hearing is pretty dull compared with that of a bass. This isn't surprising. In its eat-or-be-eaten world, a bass survives mainly on its ability to detect even the most minute vibrations or sounds. And this is where a lot of fishermen fall flat on their basses. Because they don't see ears hanging off a bass's head, they either assume a bass can't hear or they give it no thought at all. If we could hear so well, we might hear a sneeze a mile away. The moment you credit the bass with super hearing ability is the moment you begin thinking like a bass. So let's begin.

The bass has a remarkable sensory system. The next time you catch one, examine it carefully. Look closely at the lateral line that runs the length of the body, slightly above center.

This entire area is made up of internal open canal systems and sub-systems. These are filled with water and thus are sympathetically attuned to any movements occurring in the bass's detection range. As we learned in chapter 3, tiny sensors, called neuromasts, function as hypersensitive, omnidirectional receptors that can interpret with unerring accuracy whether vibrations come from something the bass wants to eat, or something that might want to eat the bass.

Without these sensors a bass would never survive beyond the fingerling stage. Some species of fish use their sensors rather than their eyes as a guidance system when dashing about through brush or rocky cover. And some believe that bass use their sensors to detect passing objects in the black of night or in muddy water where vision is impossible.

I was watching a bass in Tom Mann's Fish World aquarium when he dimmed the lights. The bass's fins began moving to send out waves, bouncing them off hard objects and tracking them with its lateral line to keep from bumping into them. This process is similar to the way a sonar works: By sending out a signal and noting both the length of time and the direction the signal takes on its return, a skilled sonar operator can accurately gauge distances, identify objects, and even estimate interception points for moving targets.

Thus, even a blind bass can home in on moving objects beyond normal sight until it's close enough for the kill. Obviously, such a super-sensitive sensory system makes it easy for a bass to pick up the vibrations of our artificial lures. In fact, a bass can detect even the soft movements of a plastic worm or a jig-grub, or the flow of current around a streamer fly.

The nearest a bass comes to hearing as we do is through its inner ears, located inside its head. Sound vibrations are transmitted to the inner ears through the flesh and bone of the head.

Remember that a bass does very little hearing as you and I think of it, through the head. A bass *feels* sound vibrations, and it becomes aware of your presence long before you detect the bass. Yes, some bass are dumb and get caught early, but the majority are survivors. You need to keep this in mind when you're bass fishing. Now, let's move on to more information about sounds in the bass's realm.

Let's go back to a fascinating day I shared with one of the rare talents in the bass-lure business. George Perrin was a maker of plastic novelties in Fort Smith, Arkansas, and also a top-notch bass fisherman. Rapala had just hit big in the U.S. market, but was unable to supply the demand. Perrin decided to fill this market gap, but not in the usual look-alike fashion. He knew his hard-plastic lure would cast better than the lighter, balsa wood Rapala, but he wanted his lure to have the same allure. So Perrin invested in sophisticated equipment to analyze the Rapala. He built a huge circular tank with a picture window to view lures in motion and an aquaphone to pick up not only audible lure sounds but also their vibratory sound tracks. Attached to the aquaphone were an oscilloscope, which would produce a visible picture of a lure's sound emissions, and an oscillograph to record this as a pattern on paper.

Watching Perrin demonstrate his equipment, and having been a lure designer myself at one time, I was hit with a compelling question: If we picked the ten all-time best-selling wiggling lures and ran them through his analyzer, would their vibratory patterns share a common denominator?

Perrin made the tests and came up with this intriguing conclusion: These proven wiggling bass catchers *all* have a vibration frequency of around 2,000 cycles per minute, plus or minus a couple hundred cycles. So I had to ask the obvious question. All of us can see wiggling lures in motion, and I had read that the fastest vibrations a human eye can detect are about 80 per second. Yet his charts were showing around 2,000 vibrations per minute. How could this be?

He replied, "A swimming lure has two vibration patterns. One is a high-frequency sound we can hear, metal hooks rattling on metal hangers, in the high-frequency range. The other vibration pattern, which our eyes record, is the number of body beats per second, usually under a dozen."

One of Perrin's engineers explained it to me this way: "To distinguish between these two types of vibrations, let's picture a piano key. As you hit it rapidly to make it sound off, the tone could be vibrating in the ten thousand cycles-per-second range. But say you were hitting the key three times per second: that is the beat. So it is with swimming bass lures."

Of course, the wide variety of bass lures makes an equally wide variety of sounds: jointed bodies knocking together, BBs or lead inserts intended to rattle, the hissing of spinners, the fluttering of soft plastic worms and jig-grubs, the varied commotions of surface lures, the soft swishing of stickbaits, and the sinuously quiet motions of weedless spoons. The bass's amazing sonar system can detect them all. It's quite possible that the quieter movements of these lures could resemble the vibratory patterns of the quietly moving creatures bass feed on, such as minnows, leeches, tadpoles, and frogs.

New bass lures are forever hitting the market with big ad campaigns, and fishermen buy them. If they catch fish, they stay around for years. If they don't catch fish, they fade from the scene and join a long list of losers. Some lures have earned a spot in history as effective bass catchers, yet over time they seem to lose their hot appeal and catch bass only occasionally. Here is a theory, supported by careful studies, about why this happens.

Larger warier bass can readily detect a source of danger. If a young, impulsive bass grabs a lure and then fights to escape, older bass notice. Maybe they're warned by the struggle or perhaps by the sudden emission of lactic acid or urine. Whatever, they watch and learn.

Biologists in Texas trapped some of these wiser bass and planted them in a virgin lake. Not only were they virtually uncatchable, but they passed this wariness along to their offspring. Others studies have revealed that in newly opened reservoirs some 80 percent of the bass—the dumber, less wary fish—are caught in the first two years. The remaining bass suddenly become harder to catch. A good number are still there, but they're the older, wiser 20 percent, some of which will never be caught.

Now to that canny 20 percent. Some of these fish can be caught by unusual tactics they've never seen before or by a maneuver that triggers an impulsive strike. Some of these methods are discovered accidentally or tried in desperation. Here are some examples.

In an interview with professional bassman Bobby Murray, after he won a major B.A.S.S. tournament, I asked: "Has any unusual sound ever helped you catch more fish than usual?" He grinned and replied:

> Yes, but I don't tell many people about it because few would believe me.
>
> I was guiding a couple crappie fishermen and my old standby brush pile failed me for the first time. Usually every time we trolled past it with a small spoon or spinner, we caught crappies. I was about to give up when I leaned over and rested my rod hand on top of the electric motor.
>
> I could feel it vibrating heavily because of a bent prop. Just as we passed the brush pile we each caught a crappie. I wondered why because we had trolled this same course a half-dozen times. The only thing different was my hand on the motor.
>
> So, I circled and trolled past the brush pile again, hand on motor, and . . . three more crappies. We retrolled the same course without my hand on the motor, and no crappies. There was something about that motor vibration transmitted through my hand, down the rod and line, and into the lure which turned on those crappies!

Crappies and bass are in the same family. Makes you think a little deeper about how sensitive fish are to vibrations, hey? Well, keep on thinking and ponder this next one.

Glen Lau thinks as much like a fish as any angler I know. He had to because for fourteen years he made his living as a fishing guide on Lake

Erie. But Glen was no ordinary guide; he spent his days off prowling the bottom of the lake, studying fish and their habit patterns in a scuba outfit so that he could become the best guide on the lake.

Now Glen is one of the nation's best outdoor filmmakers, especially on bass fishing, because he knows so much about them. So I asked him how fish responded to sounds, and he came back with this intriguing memory.

I was guiding a couple of perch fishermen on Lake Erie, and the usual reef where they hung out in schools just didn't pay off. It was so slow I decided to move to another spot.

I began to pull in the Danforth anchor and heard it clank on the rocks. Immediately, all three rods started jumping with perch. We rebaited, I clanked the anchor, and three more perch. We tried no clanking and got no perch.

We sat there and clanked up three limits of perch. I tried other anchors but their sounds didn't have it; the Danforth had a different ring to it. I was able to duplicate it with a metal bar and usually—not always—could turn on enough perch for a day's catch.

Here's the point: The average angler would never connect a vibrating motor or a clanking anchor to catching fish. Bobby and Glen were alert pros and sensed the connection. Think like them!

The instant you catch a bass, the first thought through your noggin should be, *why*? Was it where you were fishing, the kind of lure you used, the way you worked it, the lure's size, action, or color? Once you figure out *why*, you should be able to repeat the successful routine.

Sound also can add an adverse dimension to catching bass. Glen was the cameraman and I the fisherman in a bass film called *Bigmouth*. We were working in the gin-clear water of Florida's Rainbow Springs. I anchored off a deep cypress-tree hole, where Glen had located some bass, and caught several nice ones for action shots. I accidentally stepped on the electric motor switch, and Glen surfaced immediately to say: "You know what? When that motor kicked in it made a loud *vooom*, and those bass reacted right away. The biggest ones were first to move into dark holes under tree roots. The smaller, dumber bass swam toward your boat."

Why? The pros use electric motors, and they catch bass close by. Perhaps that particular motor had a louder *vooom*. We later found it had a bent prop.

As I thought about this later, it occurred to me that in addition to the electric motor most bass fishermen use, most also use a sonar-type fish/depth sounder, which transmits signals in the range of 50 to 200 kilohertz. (One kilohertz equals 1,000 cycles per second.) We can't hear this, but can the larger, more sensitive bass?

Of course both of these valuable instruments are standard equipment, and we all catch bass with them. But these days when I locate a big-bass hangout, I find myself turning off both when I get within casting range. Isn't this carrying this sound thing too far?

Well, I look at it this way. Bass are a lot like people. We have our dumb ones and our smart ones. Dumb humans can live to old age because the smart ones look after their survival needs.

Bass aren't so fortunate. They live or die by their senses. The less alert ones either fall for a fisherman's lure or get eaten by a predator. We know the whoppers are out there, and chances are they know we are, too. They're too big for most predators, except us. So when I go bass fishing, I try to think as much like one of those alert old giants as I can.

Learn as much as you can about where the big old behemoths live. Once you locate a hangout, approach in a manner that puts the odds in your favor. And the greatest of all advantages is that of surprise, because once that savvy bass senses your presence, the advantage is hers. (Most big bass are females.)

If you can outsmart a few of these elder monarchs each year, your overall catch of small to medium bass is sure to pick up as well. So think sound. Think it before you go bass fishing, think it each time you approach a bass hangout, and think it before each cast. To ignore it is to underestimate your opponent, a bad tactical error in any contest. With big bass, thinking sound is, well, just sound thinking!

14 What Colors Make Bass Bite?

When serious bass anglers get together, one question always seems to get debated: Can bass tell one color from another? Some doubt it, many could care less, but I don't know one serious bass fisherman who isn't convinced that bass can not only read colors but also distinguish delicate shades of each.

I'm convinced. Bass have just flat told me they want a particular color shade in preference to another on too many occasions. Let me cite some examples.

Many times over the years a fishing buddy has begun racking up bass on a certain color combo, let's say a red head and silver body. I'd note the catching combo but wouldn't use it, because I wanted to know if that particular color combination was the only one they wanted.

I was called hardheaded and stubborn because I wouldn't put on the catching lure. I tried many combos—silver body and cardinal head, silver body and pink head, silver body and black head. I tried all other shades of red I could find plus other contrasty head colors. And often I didn't catch bass until I offered precisely the same color combo my buddy was using.

This is especially true with plastic worms, perhaps even more so than with hard lures. Sometimes I might catch bass on an odd shade of light blue, for example. I asked my partner to use it while I tried every other blue color I could find. Occasionally the other colors scored, but most of the time I was forced to revert to that peculiar shade of light blue.

For another graphic example, one time my crony was using a strip of pork rind that he had soaked in Merthiolate to give it a pinkish shade.

We were fishing weedless spoons through pockets in lily pads and the water color was tannic, about like weak coffee or strong tea.

He had the happy look of a commercial fisherman in a hole full of fish as he wrestled in one bass after another. I stuck my thumb several times, hurrying through all the other colors of pork rind I had: red, yellow, black, white, and frog green. All they elicited were swirls, no takers.

When I switched to the Merthiolated strip I had no trouble matching him bass for bass. I have tried this red-orange color many times since with poor results. On that tannic-water day, it worked!

Before we launch into the whys of such occurrences, here's one more example of bass with picky preferences. It's common to meet fishermen with half their huge tackle boxes filled with their preferred types of bass lures, such as jigs, deep-diving plugs, bucktail spinners, or top-water noisemakers. These anglers are semispecialists who prefer to fish one type of lure almost to the exclusion of anything else.

A jig-grub man will have them in all sizes and colors—hair bodies in yellows, whites, blacks, browns, plus combinations of these colors; heads of red, yellow, white, black, green, and pink. A spinner specialist may have bodies of widely assorted colors plus spinner blades in different sizes, shapes, and textures—hammered, fluted, sparkly brass, chrome, and copper. Wiggling plug fans will carry all sizes, with lips that run from shallow to deep, and a full range of colors from subtle naturals to those with sharp, contrasty combinations—all to cover every possible situation of water visibility. Here's my point: These specialists don't need to tell me that where they fish the bass demand certain lure types and specific color shades or combos. One look inside their tackle boxes speaks for itself. And I agree with them.

But there are skeptics who would say that these specialists are giving bass credit for senses and smarts that such dumb creatures couldn't possibly have. All that care about catering to their choice of the moment is pure poppycock.

Let's see what the scientific community has to say about this. I've pored over the latest studies in the realm of fishes and their responses to colors and shades of colors. We'll begin by discussing those all-important optic organs.

We know that human eyes can see colors and shades of colors, but what have they in common with a bass's eyes? A lot! Like our eyes, those of a bass have rods and cones. Rods make it possible to see black, white, and gray shades. Cones distinguish colors. And like those of humans, bass eyeballs have transparent corneas, irises, lenses, retinas, and muscles to move the eyes.

There is a slight difference in shape. A bass's eyeball is almost round except for a flattened outer surface; ours is bulged. A bass's eye focuses by using muscles to change the position of the lens; our eyes focus by changing the shape of the lens.

Further, actual measurements of the focal distance of a bass's eye compared with that of a human eye reveal an increase in lens curvature that lets in five times more light. This curvature is important in the dimly lit world of the bass. We don't need it in our bright realm.

And here's a clincher: Human eyes contain a substance called *rhodopsin*, without which we would see only black, white, and shades of gray—no colors. A bass's eye contains rhodopsin, too.

So according to opthamologists, the bass is fully equipped to see color. As for shades of colors, let's delve into some studies on the subject. For these papers I am indebted to Ed Keller, retired specialist on bass studies, once public relations director with Du Pont's monofilament line division.

In controlled laboratory tests, bass were fed mosquito larvae and daphnia, a type of water flea, using eye-droppers of various opaque colors and hues. Interestingly, the bass preferred red and yellow over all other colors—the two all-time best bass-catching colors.

How do we know the bass weren't responding to light-wave frequencies and not color? Each color was tested against an entire range of grays, from stark white to jet black. Gentle shocks were administered on certain shades of red, ranging from bright scarlet to pale pink. The bass avoided the shock-related hues and responded to the nonshocking ones.

Further tests proved that bass can distinguish twenty-four different narrow-band hues; some even exceed man's spectral vision range into the violets. The researchers concluded that bass respond to colors about the same way we do when wearing yellow-tinted glasses. We who wear yellow Polaroids on dark days know how these intensify existing light and most colors.

These conclusions come as no surprise to veteran bass fishermen, who have been catching bass on pastel-shade lures for years. But it's good to have a theory backed up with facts.

Now let's switch from the laboratory, where the lights are bright and the water clear, to the realm of the bass, where light varies from bright to blackout. Looking down through the water toward bottom, where fish and cover are plainly visible, we might think that the water is very clear. But go down there with scuba gear and look horizontally, and you'll find visibility much more limited, mostly because of the algae concentrations common to most fertile bass waters. A bass's eyes are five times more effective at gathering light than ours, however, and bass can see well enough to find food and hit lures, especially those with contrasting colors.

To get some idea of how colors appear under water, scientist Paul Johnson and I made a series of tests in the crystal-clear waters of Rainbow Springs, Florida. Paul was in the water in scuba gear while I observed and photographed through the portholes of a special underwater craft. We wanted to see if the camera's sensitive and impartial eye

Paul Johnson is a most dedicated specialist on bass behavior, and I had the privilege to work with him in the crystal-clear waters of Florida's Rainbow Springs. Here a bass appears to be talking with him; as he studied them they learned he was friend, not foe, and became quite chummy. Here we learned why blue and purple are the best bass-catching colors nationally: they're the most discernible at the greatest distances.

would confirm on color film what our eyes and judgment decided. Surprisingly, both came close.

Most lures are opaque and plastic worms are translucent, so Johnson used a rod to suspend various colors of plastic worms and another to suspend plastic color chips in all popular lure shades. He started close to my porthole and slowly walked away while I observed and made notes. The most-popular bass lure color, red, remained red until almost out of sight, then it turned black. Red stood out in stark contrast against any background—weeds, sky, or bottom.

Yellow, the second most popular bass color, turned whitish shortly before red turned black, but remained visible much farther than white and far past where red disappeared completely. Chartreuse topped plain yellow for distance and stood out in sharp contrast against all backgrounds. But an offbeat color—a bright robin's-egg blue—was the most visible of all, sharply discernible as light blue far past yellow; it finally turned off-white just before fading into nothingness. And yet there's never been a hot-selling light-blue lure. Maybe lure makers decided no one would buy it. I wonder if the bass would?

Now, let's review our tests on the all-time best-catching artificial bass lure, the soft-plastic worm. Because of their translucence in some colors, the worms told a different story.

Red held its vivid color almost as far as it could be seen, then faded into maroon and, finally, black before it disappeared. Like the red chip, it was contrasty against all backgrounds.

Yellow, which is only a mediocre seller in worms, was the brightest and most contrasty under all light conditions. Perhaps this is why it doesn't catch bass as well as other colors; maybe it's too visible. I find myself reaching for a yellow worm only under adverse visibility conditions. But when used in the tail only, yellow does produce regularly in off-color water or dim light.

Now for the surprise: Thinking bass fishermen long have wondered why blue and purple are the two best-selling worm colors nationally. As we took the worms deeper, suspended side by side to get a comparison of color visibility, we got an inkling. As most bass fishermen have learned, the deeper you go into a normal bass lake, the dimmer the light becomes. The colors of the spectrum that penetrate deepest are the ultraviolets, and these seem to do something to blue and purple plastic worms that makes them extremely visible compared to other, even brighter colors.

In average bass water, where the visibility ranges from a few inches to a couple of feet to human eyes, and possibly a foot to 2 or 3 to a bass's eyes, blue and purple plastic worms retain their true color as far as they can be seen. Just before disappearing, they still appear to be dark blue or violet. Compared with other colors, bass should be able to see them better.

To generalize, in hard lures the reds, yellows, and contrasty shades are best most of the time in all water conditions. With plastic worms or other soft, translucent lures, stay with the blues and purples in clear water, but try brighter colors in low-visibility conditions.

In summary, remember this: The world of the angler is normally bright and well lit; the world of the bass is dim and murky. No one *really* knows which color will tempt bass, given all the variations in light penetration, water clarity, visibility, and the changeable moods of these predators. No one except the bass, that is. Remember the above information on color contrasts and recognition, and work it into your presentations, but keep changing lures, colors, and tactics every ten to twenty-five casts and let the bass tell you if all these well-meant tests have any meaning. When they do, think how smart you'll feel for having tried them!

Photograph by Glen Lau.

15 Bass Secrets Revealed—by Bass

Most seasoned, savvy bass fishermen know that "finding the pattern of the moment" is the most important factor in catching bass. What they don't know is that most seasoned, savvy bass already have the fisherman's pattern, and buzz off the instant they detect his presence.

For years, wiser fishermen have tried to be super-quiet lest a bass hear the noise of their boat, oars, anchor, motor—even loud talking. But *even this* isn't wise enough. Studies have revealed that just the intrusion of an artificial lure can spook a wary bass and kill the chance to catch that fish.

I was privileged to witness how these studies were conducted with the latest scientific gear in the hands of a dedicated biologist, Mike Lembeck, who for two years systematically studied bass behavior in well-managed bass lakes in the San Diego area. The study was funded by the San Diego County Fish and Wildlife Committee, and they are to be commended for their efforts. His findings have made me a much wiser bass angler.

In Lembeck's studies, 147 largemouth bass were observed in wild habitat, with the bass unaware they were under surveillance. Lembeck surgically implanted into each bass's abdominal cavity a miniature radio transmitter, similar to the system used for years to study sharks and whales. Continuing advances in the miniaturization of electronic components led to the production of transmitters small enough for freshwater species. Each transmitter was tuned to have a different beep count. By timing, say, 20 beeps with a stopwatch, it is possible to positively identify each bass.

I watched as Lembeck lowered over the side of our boat a directional hydrophone—an underwater microphone that registers the strongest signal when pointed directly at the transmitter. It looks very much like a padded funnel at the end of a broomstick.

Listening through earphones and pointing the hydrophone toward shore, Lembeck studied his watch as he counted beeps, then looked in his notebook and said: "The bass we have located is a male, two and a half years old, and it's about six feet to the right of that brush pile. And it weighs about four pounds."

"How do you know that a bass carrying a metal transmitter in its innards is reacting like a wild bass?" I asked.

"Here's how," Lembeck replied. "By repeated observations we know that transmittered bass, on several occasions, have fed within two days after surgery. Five bass were captured two to three weeks after being transplanted and all were in excellent condition, totally healed.

"And here's the clincher," he added. "To prove normal behavior, records show that bass with transmitters were caught at the same rate as bass without them. You see, the transmitter is only two-and-a-half inches long and requires only a one-inch incision. And the entire operation takes less then ten minutes, so it's not a debilitating experience."

Each bass was pinpointed by triangulation, and as many as thirty bass in one reservoir were followed at one time. Their locations were marked on a topographic map, and several different males were planted closely enough to be caught from their nests to record pertinent data. And mark this: Bass were located 99.8 percent of the time!

The testing took place in six San Diego reservoirs. Most of the plantings were made in El Capitan and San Vicente reservoirs, and the bass ranged from a small 1¼-pounder to a 14-pound giant. To set the scene for these studies, let's take a close look at these reservoirs and their makeup to help you relate them to lakes near you.

El Capitan is a fairly deep body of water with about 500 surface acres. The water is slightly murky, and there's some 10.7 miles of shore cover. El Cap's open to the public three days weekly from fall to spring. This is very intelligent planning, keeping fishing pressure at a low level and giving bass a chance to forget the sounds of anglers.

San Vicente is deep, clear, and some 950 acres in area, with 16 miles of shoreline, including an island in the center with 2 miles of shore. The structure is rocky, and it's open to public fishing four days weekly from early fall to late spring.

Female bass are the gadabouts

Bass tend to follow individualistic patterns, but the two-year study showed that, in general, the females do most of the roaming. Their movements show two distinct modes. Some bass prefer to travel along shorelines, close in, while others that journey farther choose open water. It was common for big females to move two to three miles, with a daily average of about a half mile. At times they coursed the entire length of El Capitan about twice weekly.

Males stayed put, especially during the spring before and after spawning. They did not begin moving until about July, even though their spawning activities were over. Winter was their season to gallivant. For most of the year there were three main activity periods—morning, noon, and sundown.

Depth preferences

Using a depth sounder in conjunction with his aquaphone, Lembeck was able to register the depths the bass preferred. These varied during the day, but once a bass chose a depth for food or sanctuary, it stayed with it.

There were marked depth preferences within the two lakes through the year. In El Capitan, with less clarity and depth, bass stayed at shallow 6- to 12-foot levels from January through May. In early June they moved down to deeper levels, 12 to 22 feet. Water normally stratifies, with the thermocline at 22 feet.

In San Vicente's deeper, clearer waters bass sought levels similar to those in El Capitan. However, when the lake went through the early winter turnover and the temperature was the same from top to bottom, bass hung out at 35- to 60-foot depths. The colder the winter, the deeper bass stayed. So check out your lakes seasonally, and keep notes on where the bass prefer to stratify.

The sun and weather

One of the more surprising notes in Lembeck's journal was that bass showed no noticeable preference for or aversion to sunlight. They didn't select the shady side of structure nor did they go deeper to avoid bright sunlight. This is contrary to the beliefs of many fishermen, who prefer to fish dark, shady areas, thinking that bass prefer them.

Bass also showed no reaction to stormy weather, with heavy rain and gusty winds up to 25 miles per hour—even those bass in shallow water or on windy shores. In other words, the bass's realm is little disturbed by our worldly elements.

Seasonal hangouts

At certain times of year bass showed definite preferences for some areas, especially in El Capitan's murkier waters. During December they sought out deeper, longer arms but avoided them the rest of the year. During January they went for the shallows and stayed there until mid-June, then headed for deeper water until early November.

Preferred cover

Some 73 bass were charted in 200 spots along El Cap's lengthy shoreline. Most of these hangouts were the kind you and I would choose to fish: brush, rocky outcroppings, points, etc. Others were less obvious: a single stickup weed tip, a couple of small protruding rocks, a steep drop-off shore, an underwater ledge, or a shoal below the surface. One thing stood out, however: Some bass preferred weeds, others brush or rocks, and they spent much of their time here.

Noncover bass

In both lakes (somewhat more in El Capitan), some bass were constantly charted away from shore or any type of cover. Some spent a day or two, some months. They consistently moved around searching for schools of shad, which showed up on the sonar.

Apparently only the spawning urge brought these bass shoreward. Why these certain bass had the open-water urge is a mystery, but perhaps it's related to why some human tribes are nomadic while others prefer to remain in one area. Knowing there are nomadic bass like these, a good sonar could help you locate them year-round.

Bass know our patterns, too

When Lembeck first began tracking bass, curiosity moved him to see how successful he'd be at catching them. From the beginning, when lures were cast to the majority of these fish, they quickly moved out of the area.

The few cases when bass didn't spook at the appearance of a lure occurred around heavier cover, usually with what appeared to be nesting males. Such bass are aggressive because they're protecting their territory from the menacing lure, not attacking it because of hunger.

Curious, I asked Lembeck to locate a big bass and let me try a different approach to see if it would make a difference. He checked his log and said, "Over there by that brush pile is a female bass around 5 pounds, been there a couple years. Give her a go!"

I dug into my box and came up with a 4-inch plastic worm, impaled it on a jighead, rigged it on an ultralight outfit with 4-pound line, and cast it well beyond her brush pile. I crawled it slowly over the bottom until I judged it opposite her hangout, then hopped it off the bottom.

Lembeck still had his aquaphone in the water and he suddenly turned it sideways, saying, "There she goes, about 75 feet down that shore. It wouldn't matter what you offered that bass; she would take off the instant anything foreign comes into view. That bass is either a coward or a supreme survivor. I'd choose the latter."

Lembeck's study proves that there are some bass that can be caught, and some that will never be caught, regardless of the angler's skill. But that's good: Those bass help maintain the population!

I salute Mike Lembeck and dedicated biologists like him. Through them we learn things about our favorite gamefish we'd otherwise never know. Many of these things sharpen our kinship with the wondrous wild creatures God created for man to ponder and enjoy.

16 The Invader Concept for Lunker Bass

E ver catch a 10-pound bass? Few fishermen have. Bud Andrews has, though—327 bass over 10 pounds—all on artificial lures. Andrews runs a guide service on Florida's Kissimmee River chain and has built his business as a trophy bass specialist. He and I went fishing, and he agreed to share his special methods with you.

Andrews's theory may be radical, but I believe it to be the most insightful I've heard for outwitting lunker bass on artificial lures. His methods may challenge your patience and credulity and shatter some of your old habits, but if you'll take the time to master his techniques, I gay-ron-tee you'll catch the biggest bass that live wherever you fish. It won't be easy. I'm still struggling!

Andrews says the theory grew on him one night as he pondered the number of times he had sipped a pop and eaten a sandwich while his lure laid on the bottom. Suddenly the line would move out, he'd grab the rod, set the hook, and a monster bass would be on the other end. Thus was born the invader concept!

The theory

Some bass live long enough to become huge by being much more wary than other bass. To survive for twelve to eighteen years, depending on latitude, they had to learn to avoid the usual offerings of today's "cast-and-run" fishermen. And they see a lot of this type!

Using their sensitive sonar system, these wise old bass detect the countless artificial lures that land nearby. They get so used to this pattern

Bud Andrews, lunker bass specialist, also guides and shares his lore with every client—leaving them sharper bass anglers—and he urges them all to release their bass and get fiberglass replicas.

that they ignore the comings and goings of lures. They can feed whenever they're ready and so have no need to chase such fleeting things.

But picture this: A critter lands somewhere within a 25-foot radius, and the big bass's sonar system pinpoints it instantly. But unlike the usual pattern, this time it doesn't run away. Uh-oh, this is different. A creature has invaded her territory and is hanging around. Her sonar receptors are on full alert. This is a challenge from an alien, and she is compelled to find the intruder and carefully check it out.

Methodology

Here's your first discipline. Don't cast directly into a bass's hangout, but 10 to 15 feet away from it. And let the lure lie there for five to ten minutes, no movement whatsoever. This is the toughest part of the invader system, the waiting. Sixty percent of the attacks occur during this wait.

After a torturous wait, at times up to fifteen minutes, Andrews reels slack out of his line, raises the rod tip, and nudges the lure into motion. He sits on ready, all senses alert. Some pickups occur now. If not, another nudge, and another five- to ten-minute wait. Another nudge, and if nothing happens, Andrews tries a new spot.

When a bass takes the lure, here's your second discipline—one completely contrary to the patterned habits of 90 percent of today's best bass anglers. Instead of quickly reeling slack out of the line and setting the hook pronto, pull slack line from your reel so that the bass feels absolutely no resistance. Andrews has found that tension in the line will cause a wary whopper to blow out the lure immediately.

Keep the rod tip low and stay ready. The wait seems interminable at times but you must let the bass pull the line taut before setting the hook with gusto. Andrews believes that most big bass are lost when the angler tries to set the hook too soon, with a self-defeating bow in the line.

The deadly trio

Most of this expert's bass have come on three popular types of lures. The number-one producer is a 7¼-inch plastic worm, rigged weedless on a No. 4 Mustad or Tru-Turn hook kept honed to a fine point. Dark colors do better on bright days, light ones on dark days. His choice of bullet sinkers is ⅛ ounce on 10-pound line and ¹⁄₁₆ ounce on 8-pound line.

His number-two catcher is a slim-minnow floater. Most bass take these as they lie still on the surface. A small percentage attack as he slowly retrieves the lure with minute twitches.

The third best producer is a lipless crankbait with internal rattles. After each cast he leaves this sinking lure lying still on the bottom, and this is when most pickups occur. He nudges it only after five to ten minutes of doing nothing.

THE HANGOUTS

Here are the spots Andrews seeks as he scours a new lake for big-bass hangouts: reeds, cattails, bulrushes, lily pads, maiden cane, peppergrass, hydrilla, milfoil, or brush. As you move along a shoreline, keep your eyes coursing for any movement, especially big, sudden swirls.

The outside edge of shore cover bordering deep water is prime territory that big bass regularly patrol. Ideal depths are 6 to 15 feet. The inside edge of habitat where dark water indicates good depth is another choice hangout, especially washtub-size pockets. Also dependable are steep drop-offs along riprap shores, off rocky-sloping points, around midlake reefs or humps, and in deep eddy water where a stream pours into a lake.

The best times of year are early spring, when bass activity is at its height, and late summer, when the first cool nights of fall bless our climate.

What did Andrews do with all those gigantic bass? He mounted the first ten for his office wall and released the rest. He allows his clients to keep only one trophy bass. I salute him!

17 The Slim Minnow, All-Purpose Lure

One question often comes up in bass-angler gabfests: If you could have only one bass lure for all over America, which one would it be? The winner invariably is the slim minnow. Oh, plastic worms give it plenty of opposition, but lose out because the slim minnow can be fished top to bottom. The worm spends all of its time on or near bottom.

Slim minnows have been on the market for more than a half century in varied forms, but it wasn't until 1962 that it came into its glory. That's when a Finnish lure made by Lauri Rapala (pronounced *Rap*-ala not Ra-*pala*) was featured in a *Life* magazine article as a lure fish couldn't resist.

Since the Finns couldn't meet the demand for their handmade lure, American lure makers brought out several versions. The most successful copy was the Rebel, made by a company of the same name. And it made the company.

Both lures are still top sellers for one good reason: they catch bass, as well as every other species of gamefish. And they catch them in so many ways one is bound to work for you. My tackle box always holds a wide selection of patterns and sizes of slim minnows. Let me share with you some of my tactics for fishing this versatile lure.

Nothing, absolutely nothing, tempts a reluctant bass quicker than an injured minnow in its death throes. And with its buoyancy, shape, and quick, wiggly action, nothing better imitates an injured minnow than the slim minnow. Here's how to do it.

First, attach a slim minnow using a snap to provide maximum free-dom of movement and make it easy to change lures. Cast it near shore cover you know holds bass, then make it do the things a dying minnow does, like quiver. To imitate *the quiver,* reel slack out of the line and with a tiny movement of the rod tip, barely nudge the lure to life. Repeat this a half-dozen times, and if no bass bashes it, try another spot.

Then there's *the twitch*—just enough rod-tip animation to pull the minnow barely under the surface with several quick wiggles. Twitch it, then give it slack to let the minnow bounce back to the surface. This imi-tates a dying minnow that still has enough energy to dart from time to time. Let it rest for about ten seconds between twitches. Most strikes will come just as you twitch it under or the instant it bobs back to the surface.

Next, let's try *the spurt.* This imitates a minnow with a little more life left, as if it's trying to escape the danger zone. Reel all slack out of your line, pointing the rod tip toward the lure, then make a long sweep with the rod tip. The minnow will dive quickly with plenty of vibration and sound from the rapid rattling of hooks—quite audible to the bass's sensitive sonar system.

After each sweep, let the slim minnow float back to the surface and lie there for about a ten-count. Repeat for a half-dozen casts, and if it doesn't bring a bass finning for the kill, move on to another hangout.

Now, try *the sinking flutter.* Minnows die down deep, too. And a lot may be dying at the same time, injured in a feeding frenzy by a school of gamefish. When a pack of bass attacks a school of minnows, they don't just eat one at a time. Those predators dash through the bunched-up school with slashing jaws and flashing tails, leaving dozens of wounded and dying minnows in their wake, which the bass then eat at their leisure. It's up to you to make your lure look like one of these deep-down dying minnows, ready for eating. There are a couple of ways to do it.

One way is to use a sinking version of the slim minnow. Rapala has a model called CountDown, which is cleverly weighted and balanced to sink very slowly to whatever depth bass might be suspended.

Or you can make your own sinking minnow by adding weight. A handy way to do this is with SuspenDots—small, metallic dots with adhe-sive backing. Merely stick enough onto the lure to sink it slowly, keeping them along a centerline to maintain the lure's natural attitude and action.

Alternatively, you can add enough split-shot about 6 inches ahead of the minnow to slowly sink it.

Ideally you should have sinking slim minnows in at least three sizes, from 3 to 5 inches in length, to appeal to different year-classes of bass.

The countdown method allows you to fish specific depths. Time your lure to determine its sink rate. Say it's a foot in two seconds. Try counting it down to 5-, 10-, and 15-foot depths, until it's just over bottom. Retrieve with darts like a scared minnow at all depths.

Jolting is a tactic best used when the water surface is a tad too choppy for twitching and quivering quieter surface lures. Jolting will bring bass from surprising distances; I've seen them come from 75 feet!

Cast a slim minnow next to shore cover, reel slack out of the line, and point the rod tip slightly to the right of the lure. At the instant you jerk sideways with the rod tip, give the reel handle a very quick half-turn. The lure will plunge under with an unusually violent commotion—jolting—and bass can hear it far back in heavy cover. Repeat the maneuver at least six times, with 10-second pauses in between, to give the bass time to find it. Jolting is also effective in off-color water, where bass will be feeding more by hearing than by sight. Just keep moving around shorelines and jolting. The savagery of the strikes will raise your spirits and eyebrows!

Another tactic is *humping*. Do this by slowly upping the speed of your retrieve until the swimming lure humps the water—neither on top nor below, but barely under the surface and making a soft V-wake as it hurries along.

Work it parallel to shore cover and 5 to 10 feet distant. Keep it coming, and you'll note the shock waves from the humping minnow fanning out 15 to 25 feet behind the lure, rippling their way into the shore cover where bass are lurking. Bass feel these vibes and come dashing out to see what kind of critter is humping along.

Bottom browsing is a technique that imitates the way small baitfish feed. Ever go skin diving and watch shad, shiners, or small bluegills grubbing along the bottom for food? Their attitude is nose down, tail up. To a bass, this vertical feeding attitude means meal time, too, because these food fish are focused on the bottom, not on lurking predators.

You can rig your slim minnow to fish just over bottom weeds, like a dumb little fish waiting to be eaten. You'll need a selection of the bullet-shape slip sinkers used for fishing plastic worms Texas-style, in ¹⁄₁₆-, ¹⁄₈-, ³⁄₁₆-, ¹⁄₃-, ³⁄₈-, and ¹⁄₂-ounce sizes. Tie on a slim minnow, then begin hanging slide sinkers on the front treble hook until you find the weight that sinks the lure fairly quickly. Place this sinker on the line ahead of the lure and ease it into the water alongside the boat. It should sink the minnow fast enough to make it wiggle on descent. If it doesn't, add the next heavier weight. Too much weight is better than too little, so take the time to be certain the minnow reacts quickly when the weight of the sinker pulls it down.

Search for deeper water in offshore spots that border on cover, plus shoals, reefs, and humps in 10- to 30-foot depths. You need to "feel out" those with weedy bottom cover. You can tell by the way your lure reacts. Here's the technique. Fling out your longest cast and let the sinker take the slim minnow down until slack line tells you it has bottomed. Draw the lure toward you with your rod tip and be alert to the feel of weeds holding it back.

Bill Dance, popular fishing TV host and tournament-fishing great, lets me land his bass for the camera. Bass were not in shore cover and eluded us until Dance put on a Carolina rig with a 1-ounce ball sinker. I asked "Why so heavy? A half-ounce will sink the lure?" Dance replied, "Well, Uncle Homer, I want it to hug the bottom so that when I lift and drop it, the lure will make a quick dart to the bottom, as if feeding." The picture proves his wisdom was right on, and most of our bass came from this rig, using a slim-minnow lure.

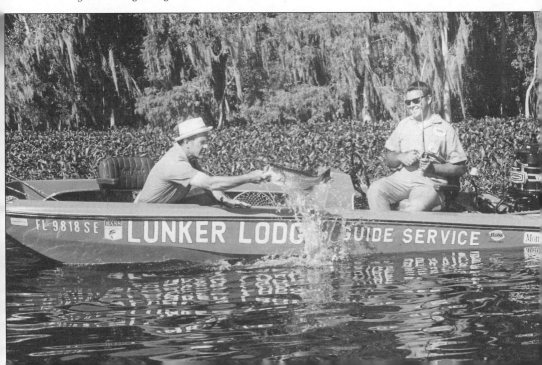

Now comes the final adjustment. You need to know the height of the weeds to get your lure working nose-down just above them, like a foraging food fish. Force the point of a toothpick into the hole of the slip sinker about a foot above the lure. Make another long cast and let the lure settle to the bottom. Now draw the lure toward you; it should be easy to tell if it's still dragging against weed tips. If so, slide the slip sinker about 2 feet above the lure.

Keep adjusting the sinker height until you no longer feel the weeds pulling against the lure. This is the proper adjustment for those particular weeds. Break off the toothpick, leaving just a small piece to wedge the sinker in place. Now when you draw on the lure, the sinker will be dragging through the weeds, stirring up sediment, and the lure will be wiggling above and behind it, looking like a feeding food fish.

One word of caution. This tactic will catch bigger bass, because they spend most of their time in bottom weeds. So be certain your line is fresh and adequate, your knot strong, and your rod gutsy enough to stand a hefty battle. It could produce your all-time biggest bass!

Well, that wraps up our coverage of slim-minnow lures, one of fishing's all-time best bass catchers. I know one professional guide who has nothing but slim minnow lures in his tackle boxes—all sizes, weights, colors, and depths. Now that's what I call a vote of confidence from an expert who makes his living fishing for bass!

18 Put the Buzz on Bass

When bass fishermen first saw buzzbaits clattering over the surface, looking like a mini–electric mixer half out of the water, they shook their heads in disbelief. Now they bless the inventor who concocted them!

The buzzbait has become one of the all-time best big-bass catchers, one that can turn lazy lunkers into savage smashers on days when nothing else works. This wondrous family of topwater spinners has come on strong in the past five years. Yet the concept has been around since the early 1930s.

The first buzz-type lure I recall using regularly was called the Sputterfuss, which is still on the market. I remember the first time I used it, too. It was somewhere around 1944. The water was calm and so was my redheaded bass buddy—until I buzzed my Sputterfuss over the surface.

"Whatinell you tryin' t'do?" he exploded. "That thing'll scare the scales off bass. Put it away!" Several casts later a bass blasted it, and he snorted: "Well, that's one crazy bass you won't need to scale—and I still can't believe it!"

The first time I heard the term "buzzbait" was in 1966. A Tulsa bass club had coined the word to describe a method of fast-reeling an overhead spinner lure so that it ran barely submerged, with the spinner making a hump in the water and leaving a turbulent trail. I wrote an article about it for *Sports Afield* called "Buzzing for Bass."

Today, baits are designed just for buzzing. The spinner doesn't submerge, but remains plainly visible and very audible as it squeals, clicks,

Buzzing for bass, considered by some to be a recent method, was being done by Oklahoma's Tulsa Bass Club in the mid-1960s. Member Bud Bruce showed me how to buzz an overhead spinnerbait through heavy cover, and it often got snagged on wood. To combat this, he used 50-pound line and wore a protective glove on his left hand so he could yank the lures free. It was "cast and yank" most of the time, but worth all the effort for the quality of the bass being caught.

clatters, purrs, spits, or sputters over the surface, depending on the design of the propeller blades.

The most popular type of buzzing spinner has two heart-shaped blades with the blade tips bent upward in opposite directions. These noisily churn over the surface, spewing drops of water in all directions.

Imaginative lure designers have added many variations. In one type, the spinner blades are designed to barely contact the main shaft, producing a loud clicking sound. Another type has a metal fin protruding upward from the main wire; the revolving blade strikes it to produce a clacking splutter. Another design emits a high-pitched squeal as the blade bearing turns on a frictional shaft. Some produce a purring sound from triple blades made of lightweight plastic. All spit and splutter to varying degrees, depending on how the angler manipulates the lure.

Some buzzers are designed to float, meaning they can be fished over weeds that would entangle sinking-type buzzbaits. Floating buzzbaits can be worked very slowly and are good for times when bass decide they're not chasing fast-moving lures that day.

Sinking buzzbaits can be manipulated in several ways, depending on the mood of the bass and the instincts of the angler. The most popular method is to cast a buzzer past visible bass cover such as lily pads, weeds, brush, cattails, stickups of many types, and boat docks, using a variety of retrieves.

Some buzzbaits have a planing head to make them surface quickly for slower fishing. Others are heavier for casting into wind; these sink quickly and must be retrieved rapidly to keep them on top. How do you choose which to use?

You don't. You let the bass tell you which type of retrieve they prefer at the moment. Not only do you try retrieving at slow, medium, and fast speeds, but you also offer a variety of lure sizes, sounds, and personal touches to determine which is the key to the bass's mood.

Why do buzzbaits trigger strikes when they look unlike anything bass eat? All we can do is theorize. One educated guess is that the noisy turbulence of the propeller blade obscures the form of the lure. It looks like an intruder into the bass's domain, so it attacks.

Another guess is that since a buzzbait's antics are unlike anything a bass has seen, it strikes out of curiosity or predatory instinct. Also, because of the extremely strong shock waves emanating from the huge blade, bass are attracted from farther distances than they would be by quieter lures. Whatever the reason, if you aren't fishing buzzbaits, you may be missing the biggest bass of your life.

Acquire a half-dozen basic types and sizes. Color is of minor importance; sound is the key. Read the following tips, add your own innovations, and I bet you'll become another addicted buzzbaiter!

Tips and tricks

The more you fish buzzbaits, the more you'll come to appreciate not only their catchability but also their versatility. Here are some observations that will help smooth out some learning wrinkles.

- **Foul-ups:** Some skirted buzzbaits have tendrils so long that they tangle with the spinner blade. Just trim the offending tendrils until the fouling stops. Also, plastic blades tend to bind from aging or corrosion. When this happens, polish the shaft with steel wool, then lubricate with oil.

- **Fine-tuning:** Most buzzbaits are made on a wire frame that occasionally distorts and binds the blade. You can adjust these by bending the blade until it is in line with but not touching the main shaft. If it's a clicking-type blade, it should barely touch the main shaft.

- **Presentation:** Practice casting buzzers at home until you can drop low, flat casts onto a garbage can lid at 20 to 30 feet. This soft touchdown doesn't spook bass and may even trigger some into striking. Reel in at slow, medium, and fast cadences, but keep it coming, and be ready.

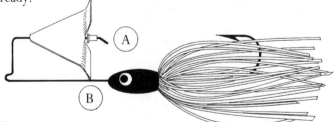

Fine-tuning
By bending down the spinner wire A, *a blade can be made to barely tick against the main shaft* B, *making sounds audible to bass up to 75 feet away.*

- **Hook setting:** Because buzzbaits are unlike other surface lures, you might lose more fish than usual. When a bass takes a buzzbait, sometimes you'll hear a loud slurp. This happens as a bass tries to inhale the lure from the surface and sucks in air with water. Here are two ways to minimize misses: You can add a single trailer hook, the same size as the one on the lure; and to give the bass time to get the hook into its maw, quickly lower your rod tip for a one-two-three count after a strike, then set the hook.

- **Adequate line:** Strong line is often necessary to haul bass out of heavy cover. The newer braided lines are ideal for this; you can have the strength of 40-pound line with the casting ease of a 12. The newer fused braids are more durable than mono around heavy cover.

- **Storing:** Cramming a tackle box full of big buzzbaits is not the way to go. They're hard to handle and easily bent out of tune. Find a tackle box with slotted, upright panels that suspends baits by their hooks, free from tangle.

- **Bearing trick:** When a buzzbait acts sluggish, polish the bearing by giving it a shot of WD-40 and letting the blade buzz in the breeze as you motor to the next hole.

- **Getting back under:** Try this sneaky tactic for bass hangouts usually impossible to reach, like way back under docks or overhanging branches. Say you're retrieving along the right side of a dock, and you want to make your buzzbait run to the left under the

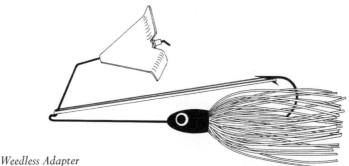

Weedless Adapter
By attaching a rubber band from the eye bend to
the hook barb, a buzzer can be made weedless for heavy cover.

dock. As you look at the bait from the front end, bend the spinner blade wire the way you want the buzzer to run (in this case to the left) so that it no longer lines up with main body wire. For best results, have both a left- and a right-hand runner handy in your tackle box. You'll be able to fish bass hangouts no one else has fished—except a smart buzzer like you!

19 Blade Lures: Underused Bass Bagger

Ever use a blade lure? Chances are you have, but not for very long. No lure hangs up more on lines, rod tips, or weeds. Yet it is one of the easiest of the all-metal lures to cast, especially into heavy winds, and one of the deadliest as well. The key to its success—and problems—lies in its design: a marriage of jighead and a flat metal minnow-shaped body with several line-tie positions to control depth and degree of wiggle. It is a vibrating phenomenon, but it's prone to hang-ups because its pair of treble hooks dangle openly under the body. Well, they may hang up on everything, but they also hang a lot of bass. This versatile lure is one of my most reliable last-ditch bass catchers.

The blade lure was the brainchild of Conrad Wood, a genius lure designer in the early 1950s. The first time I used his Sonar, I caught a limit—of snags *and* bass. It's been one of my tackle-box mainstays ever since. If you take time to develop a feel for its vibratory range and learn how to work it over various types of cover, I predict it will become one of your mainstays as well. Here are some fundamentals to remember.

To minimize tangles with line or rod tip, reel the lure tight against the tip-top before laying down a rod; don't let the lure dangle. To reduce hang-ups while fishing, don't use a blade lure inside weeds, brush, lily pads, or other entangling cover. Reserve it for open areas, over bottom cover, off rocky or riprap shores and points, and outside covers bordering dark water.

This was one of many bass that took a vertically jigged lure in 30 feet of water in a midlake locale. The guide pinpointed a drop-off on his sonar, and the two hottest lures were the blade and jighead minnow types. The payoff maneuver was barely activating the lures in a tight circle, just over bottom.

Blade lures come in assorted colors and in sizes from 1/16 through 3/4 ounce. I suggest you carry a couple of each size in contrasty colors, including gold and silver metallics and natural minnow finishes. Use light casting rigs with 8-pound line for the smaller ones and a medium-weight rig with 12-pound line for the larger sizes. Line test doesn't make much difference in the action, but don't tie the line directly to the lure. To maximize the free, wiggling action, use a round-eye snap—not a snap swivel, which tends to entangle the rear hook.

Here are time-proved blade-lure tactics that have paid off countless times for Uncle Homer.

Humping

Practice until you can make a long, soft cast. Just as the lure touches down, raise your rod tip and begin reeling just fast enough to keep the blade lure wiggling barely under the surface. This makes a vibrating ridge on the surface, like a critter running for its life, and bass will come from distant cover to attack it.

Shallowing

On shallow bottoms over rocky or weedy cover, keep your rod tip high and the blade lure lightly contacting cover throughout the retrieve. On a three-hole blade lure, use the rear hole for the shallowest running angle.

Bottoming

Where water drops off sharply into darker depths, cast a blade lure close to the cover edge and "count it down" until the line goes slack. Say it bottomed on a ten-count. Count down the next cast and begin your retrieve on a count of eight to keep the lure coming just over cover.

Slope hopping

Where a rocky shore stairsteps into deep water, cast shoreward and nudge the blade down the slope, lifting and fluttering it with the rod tip. Also cast outward into deep water and retrieve up the slope. Finally, make long casts parallel to the shore and wiggle the lure back parallel at all depths.

Flipping

Replace treble hooks with single weedless hooks. Flip the blade lure into dense weed pockets, ease it to the bottom, then yo-yo it up and down, staying alert for subtle pickups from curious bass. Set the hook at the slightest change in feel.

Gun-'n-run

There's no better lure for working a lot of varied cover spots as you search on the move. Make long to short casts about 3 feet apart to saturate the area, then move on. This surely beats working a bassless spot all day.

Depth delving

During dog-day months, bass move to deeper water. Do likewise, seeking offshore cuts, humps, reefs, river beds, bridge abutments, and midlake islands with deep perimeters. Cover these areas with blade lures contacting bottom, with the line vertical from the rod tip. Maintain a taut line as you lift the lure off bottom, then flutter it down.

Trolling

Find a deep drop-off or break in the shoreline cover pattern, and stop the boat. Make a long cast behind the boat and let the blade settle to the bottom, motor on idle. Ease the throttle forward until the lure no longer drags on the bottom. Troll close to the cover line until a bass tries to snatch your trolling rig right out of your grip.

Current event

When stream fishing for bass, it's difficult to urge most crankbaits into action unless they're running against the current. Not blade lures. They can be worked up, across, or down current with equal facility. And here's where the multiple line-tie holes do their thing. The forward hole gives the tightest wiggle and runs deepest; the second and third holes give a wider wiggle and a shallower run. Here's how to cover a stream.

Cast upstream and begin reeling until you feel the blade lure wiggling. Maintain cranking speed until the current exerts a hard pull, then slow way down and nudge it back. Find the hole that works best with the current speed and depth. Blade fishing is a sharp way to go. Do it!

20 Fly Rodding for Bass

Fly rodding just may be the best all-around method for catching the greatest number of bass. This conviction grows on me with each passing season. And yet it's rare to see one fly rodder among thousands of bass anglers. Why?

Well, maybe it's because few tackle salesmen know much about fly fishing and therefore avoid talking about it. Or maybe it's because many fishermen believe fly fishing is only for trout.

I spent eight years as a fishing-tackle salesman, and I remember the difficulty in trying to sell fly tackle. It became a real challenge. So rather than try to convert one customer at a time, I held fly-fishing schools at the YMCA to expose large groups of interested anglers to fly fishing's fun and advantages. Many companies sent in their fly-fishing experts to do guest shots. There was poor trout fishing in the area, so we changed our methods to those more suitable for panfish and bass. And the new weight-forward lines just coming out at the time made fly casting bass bugs and poppers much easier.

Since those days, the fly rod has grown in stature and popularity as a productive bass-catching method. As a salesman I enjoyed selling it because I knew how much pleasure it would bring the angler. And in selling it, I pursued uses of the fly rod beyond its usual concept . . . especially for catching bass.

One of the first discoveries of the better bass fishermen was that there were no wet fly patterns consistently successful at catching bass.

Fly rodding for a bass. Photograph by Glen Lau.

This is a typical smallmouth bass stream; the fly fisherman is slowly drifting a wet fly in the slower current abutting the giant rock. Payoff lures here can be those that match a hatch of minnows, frogs, hellgrammites, or crawfish, retrieved as naturally as possible on bottom.

This made the challenge so great that we formed a club and made concerted efforts to develop a bass-catching fly.

Despite skilled hands and minds, none resulted. But, we did learn that bass bugging with the long rod was the very best way to catch the greatest total of bass in a given period of time.

To this day, fly-rod bass bugging is so deadly and efficient it tops anything I am familiar with. Let me give you a rundown on the basic approach to see if it draws on you.

If it does, I recommend you give it a go and watch your take of bass double, possibly triple, that of your present method. You can learn the casting skill in your backyard. Practice with a hookless bug until you can layout a flat line every time.

FLY TACKLE

Choose a fly rod 8 to 9 feet long and on the muscular side. It needs to have spine with an even overall bend from butt to tip, and it should be balanced for an 8-weight line. An L8 line, which is level overall, or a bugg-taper 8-weight will bring out the action in the rod and you'll be able to handle 30 to 40 feet of line, eventually.

Buy a moderately priced single-action reel and a 10-yard coil of 20-pound monofilament for leaders. Tie 6 feet of leader to the end of your line and, as suggested, practice bug casting in your backyard.

Start with a few basic patterns of bass bugs, made from buoyant materials such as hollow deer hair, cork, or foamed plastic. These float high and can be easily animated. My best catchers are three naturals: a mouse, a spent-wing moth, and poppers in several sizes and colors. Begin with two each in both medium and large sizes.

Bass bugging

During your first half hour of fishing, forget about catching bass and concentrate on learning how to work the bugs. To get familiar with them, tie a 6-foot leader directly to your fly rod's tip section and add a bug. Splat it down close by and study the reactions as you swim the mouse, flutter the moth, and pop the poppers.

For your initial bugging trip, stay with a 6-foot leader; that's long enough for a beginner. And keep in mind that bass are creatures of cover. Look for lily pads, weeds, rocks, tree roots, logs, stumps, pilings, and piers bordering darker, deeper water.

When waters are calm and bass are looking up for prey, now is the time for fly rodding. Floating bass bugs twitched along hyacinth edges can bring some of bass fishing's greatest thrills in explosive strikes and hand-to-fin battles.

Approach quietly and select one of your bugs. Be certain the knot you use is a strong one; if in doubt, add a keeper knot to the tip of your leader to prevent slippage. Here are ways to work each bug.

The mouse

Learn to make it do everything but squeak. When a mouse falls into the water, its only thought is to get the heck out of there. So motivate it the instant it splats down and keep it swimming steadily away from the cover. Swim it with mini-twitches of the line, pulsed by your free hand or the rod tip, occasionally stopping for a rest, then moving right along. A strike can come from the second it lands until it's only a rod's length away. Keep your rod tip low and maintain constant tension on the line so you can set the hook with a full rod sweep.

A note about buying bass bugs: You can spot a shoddily tied deer-hair bug by holding the lure head in one hand and the rear end in the other. Twist, and if the body turns on the hook, find one that doesn't.

Poppers should pop, at even the most delicate jerk. If they're improperly balanced, float too high, or have the hook eye in the wrong place, they won't give you that sharp *bloop*. Tell the dealer you want to exchange them for some that do. Then stay with these performers.

The moth

Deer hair is hollow, which makes deer-hair bugs fairly buoyant and responsive. Yet they don't float as high as cork or foam bugs, and therein lies their attraction. Many times I don't begin catching bass until the moth gets a tad waterlogged and barely floats. In this state, the lure splats onto the water much as would a live moth. And remember how a moth usually acts when it falls onto the water. It's usually too stunned by the fall to move. So let your moth lie quietly for 10 to 15 seconds. Then see how *little* you can move it.

Here's a neat technique that usually works in dead-calm water. Tap the rod butt with anything metallic—a clipper, knife, fly box, whatever. Even your thumbnail flicked against the butt cap will do it. This transmits a barely perceptible vibration to the moth that will trigger strikes from even the most wary bass. Work the moth as long as possible in one spot, making maybe a dozen twitches, then snatch it away and splat it into another hangout.

The popper

I know of no creature that makes a loud *pop* on the surface, yet at times bass bust poppers with a vengeance. Here's how to work them.

With all slack out of the line and the rod tip low, pop the popper with a terse snap of the rod tip. You can also *pop* it with sharp jerks of the line hand.

Pop the lure, and let it lie motionless. Then give it barely percep-tible nudgings. Bulldoze it over the surface with your line hand, let it lie still, then pop it again. You'll soon learn to work a popper many ways and discover the ones that work best for you.

Let's pause here to cover the fundamentals of hooking a bass on a fly rod. As mentioned, keep the rod tip low and the line taut as you work the bug. The instant you see a swirl at the lure or hear a bass bust it, tightly grip the line in your line hand and sweep the fly rod back with all the muscle you can muster. You'll quickly know if you have a hookup.

There are two ways to land a bass on a fly rod. One is simply to reel it in, letting the rod tip do the work of playing it. If the bass surges and demands line, let go of the reel handle and let the bass run against the reel's drag.

Some reels have exposed rims, so that you can gently brake the revolving spool with your free hand. I prefer this type, although they cost more, because I can sense just how much pressure to apply.

The other way to bring in a fly-caught bass is by stripping it in. Just reach up to the first guide, grasp the line, and pull it downward toward the rod handle, gripping it between the thumb and forefinger of the rod hand. Repeat these actions until you land the bass.

One advantage of stripping in line is that you'll know how far away you caught that bass. This is shown by the amount of line you have around you if you're wading, or in the boat if you're afloat. Just keep it free of tangles.

So much for bugs. Let's talk about other ways to catch bass on the versatile fly rod.

SPINNER FISHING

There's an art to fishing spinners with a fly rod. Casting a lightweight fly is relatively easy: It's just pulled along to the target by the heavy fly line. But a heavy metal spinner's another story. Instead, spool about 50 feet of

10-pound monofilament on the fly reel, tying it to the backing line. Tie on an in-line spinner in the ⅒-ounce range, and forget the overhead cast. You need to learn the art of flat casting—lobbing the lure.

Begin with about half a rod-length of line hanging down. Flick the lure to and fro and feed it line with your free hand, rod parallel with the water, until the lure is over the target. Then ease it down gently.

To retrieve, let the line slide between the thumb and forefinger of your rod hand while you steadily retrieve the lure with your line hand. Once you get the distance set, just flat-cast the spinner behind you; when it reaches the end of the line, lob it forward onto the target. With a little practice you'll do a passable job on your first trip.

Working a spinner with a fly rod is a little harder than working a bug. To keep the spinner spinning you must keep it moving, and this calls for fast-stripping the line. It'll come, though: just stay with it. You'll find it a very efficient way to cover a lot of water in minimal time. I especially enjoy this method while wading a stream. I can work a riffle or undercut bank and take bass that won't respond to plugs or live bait.

PLASTIC WORMING

Most plastic-worm anglers using casting or spinning tackle miss bass because they're tardy in detecting a pickup. Here's a fly-rod rig that gives you a super-sensitive feel, and you can detect the smallest change in worm vibes.

Use a sinking fly line and a 10-pound level leader the same length as your rod. I prefer a weight-forward line, but a level or double-taper will do. Rig a 6-inch floating worm on a single hook, and bury the hook in the worm body to make it weedless. Add a small split-shot, just enough to sink the worm, about 6 inches above the lure.

Use a lateral cast, just as with the spinner, and splat the worm close to cover where the water deepens enough to be dark. Let the worm sink to the bottom, then retrieve with sharp upward sweeps of the rod tip. As you feed the worm back to bottom with your rod tip, keep the line always under mild tension. Otherwise you might not feel a bass inhale the worm, since the split-shot tends to dampen its feel.

This is a good way to fish live nightcrawlers, too, if you don't mind using live bait. In fact, during dog days, when bass are toughest to catch, fly rodding live nightcrawlers may be the only way to score.

Coping with wind

You'll hear it said that fly fishing isn't worth a hoot when it breezes up. Well, it does makes it more work, but usually you can still find a sheltered cove to fish.

But when the wind starts gusting up whitecaps, it's no fun fighting it. So don't. Let the wind help you catch bass. Run upwind with the motor, then drift across the lake, letting the wind propel your boat quietly along. Troll with the fly rod, using a plastic or live worm, minnow, crawfish, spinner, or a small wiggling lure.

Troll one complete length of the lake, then run back to the head end and troll another course about 25 yards out from the previous one. Repeat until you have thoroughly covered the area. If there are still no bass, go home and catch up on the chores.

Double-barrel fishing

I wouldn't recommend this for all fishermen, but if you're the questing type, try this efficient tactic gleaned from a guide in Montana. He devised it to tempt bass two ways with one rod.

First, he replaced the first guide on his fly rod with a larger, spinning-type guide. If it's calm, he rigs a fly reel on the rod and fishes with his assortment of flies. If they turn up their noses at these dainty offerings, he then replaces the fly reel with a spinning type. With that larger first guide to throttle down the spinning line, the fly rod does a surprisingly efficient job of casting.

He usually bug-fishes early in the day with the fly rod when the water is calm, then switches to the spinning reel when a wind rises. He wades and totes his entire lure assortment in two small plastic boxes. And he is mighty tough to top!

I hope you've decided by now that a fly rod is useful for more than flicking flies around. Bass bugging is my favorite way to fish the fly rod, but I like to let my imagination soar and see how many ways I can utilize it bass fishing. The more you use the long rod, the more it grows on you. Try it, and on those days when hefty bass are blasting your bugs, you'll head home with a deep-down, warm feeling!

21 Fishing Afoot Versus Afloat

ishing afoot, as opposed to afloat, is the way I began pursuing bass, and I like to renew my kinship with it frequently. It's one of the most enjoyable and catching ways to spend a day afield in our grand outdoors.

There's a solid cadre of hoofing anglers who wouldn't be caught in a boat. Oh, they might use an inner-tube-type belly boat to keep from stepping into holes over their heads, but most of them make like a big heron and go for one hole, one bass at a time.

And by day's end most of these wading anglers will have racked up a decent catch of bass. But there's more to wade fishing than meets the casual eye. A lot more, if you're going to be good at it.

First, let's probe the gear of the landlubber angler. It can vary from a minimalist's outfit—a cane pole, overalls, pair of sneakers, and a rucksack containing hooks, sinkers, nightcrawlers, and tools—to the most expensive rods, reels, lines, lure kits, chest waders, and fancy belly boat. To each his own. You find your druthers by trial and error, and you learn how to get by with minimal gear: everything you're carrying gets heavier as the day wears on.

I knew one Arkansawyer who caught well over a thousand bass each year. Here was his gear: a 10-foot tubular graphite telescoping pole with 10 feet of 10-pound monofilament line. Today he'd use 40-pound braided line with 10-pound diameter and never worry about losing fish or lures. His pocket kit contained a half-dozen white chicken-feather jigs, ¼-ounce size.

He wore jeans, sneakers, and a battered straw hat. He fished the shorelines of lakes and creeks, easing that jig into every possible spot a bass could hide and swimming it gently about. On a good day he'd catch and release upwards of fifty bass, keeping only those around a pound to eat. He caught other species including trout, catfish, crappies, white bass, bluegills, and even an occasional carp on that seductive white jig. He cleaned his fish waterside and took home only tender fillets. I tried but couldn't out-eat him!

Like Zekie, you can keep it simple or make it as complex as you like. I've fished with land-bound anglers who caught bass on spinning, spincasting, baitcasting, and fly gear. Just use the outfit you prefer.

In hot weather I don't bother with waders, preferring the feel of cool water on my body. I wear ankle-high sneakers because mud won't pull them off. To keep off chiggers I pull long socks over my pant legs and spray my neck and arms with bug juice. In southern waters we have to contend with trematodes, a tiny, wormlike critter that buries its head in hair follicles. A hot shower kills them but you scratch all night.

Photograph by Glen Lau.

WADING CAUTIONS

Wade-fishing is very enjoyable because of one's closeness to the bass. But there are certain precautions to take for added pleasure and safety afoot. In addition to a lure kit, I carry long-nose pliers, wasp spray, and a belt-mounted sheath knife. Sheath knife? Yep, I'll explain why later.

The pliers are for extracting and adjusting lures; the wasp spray is for any you might encounter while shaking plugs loose from limbs. Now for the long-blade knife. Many years ago I hooked a bass much like the one in the photograph on the facing page. The moment I set the hook, I felt the line go slack.

I knew the bass either had spit out the lure or was coming toward me. So I reacted by reeling like crazy, and the instant I gained a tight line I felt that whopper bass dash between my feet, then wrap the 20-pound line around both ankles. There I stood, hog-tied, while that bass tugged the line tighter and tighter, with the water about an inch below my wader tops. I tried but couldn't break the line by kicking against it.

I reached for my handy sheath knife, took a deep breath, and bent over to cut the line. I came up soaked but safe, and at that moment, skyward zoomed a 6-pound bass; she popped her jaws, spit out my worm, and took off with a "soooo long, sucker!" What a keeper memory!

In Florida we have to contend with the alligator flea, a large, beetle-like bug with a bite so painful you shuck clothes *right then* and pluck it off. We also have to contend with real alligators. Down here you learn never to keep your fish on a stringer tied to your belt. When alligators try to steal your fish, that's one tug of war you always want to lose! But all these are minor discombobulations compared with the pleasure and sport of wade fishing.

In cold, fast streams I prefer insulated hip boots over waders, because I take fewer risks. But in ponds, lakes, and slow-flowing streams, I wear chest waders. And if the luxury of fishing from a belly boat appeals to you, take a look at some of the latest innovations. Some are large enough to carry a full-size tackle box, bountiful lunch, even an electric motor to cover maximum territory with minimal effort.

At times I drive to an untried lake or stream and just have at it, assessing each shoreline feature as it comes and judging underwater terrain by the looks of the land above water. This is a serendipitous approach, and there's a lot to be said for the pleasure in strolling the unknown. But a wiser way, especially if you're on an extended trip, is to obtain maps showing bottom contours of lakes and streams you plan to fish. You can send for an index of topo maps, which contains a detailed list of all the maps that are available from the United States Geological Survey, and then request maps by name and series. If you are not certain which maps to order, write for a free index to: USGS Information Center, Box 25286, Denver, CO 80225. Be sure to specify which state you are interested in.

With the right topo map in hand, you can select accessible areas that show the most reefs, shoals, drop-off ledges, and creek channels close to the payoff depths of 10 to 20 feet. Of course, topo maps are wise tools to use even on lakes that you've been fishing and only guessing at the bottom contours. It's better to know what's below you.

When wader fishing, I carry extra ankle-high shoes to wear on the return trip. I carry the waders over my shoulder, and by the time I reach the car my sweat-soaked clothes are fairly dry. A word of caution: little-traveled trails may conceal varmints like wasps, hornets, and bees. Those that nest in trees are fairly easy to see, but ground dwellers call for a sharp eye. Poisonous snakes are rare, but watch where you step.

I like to travel light and find it impractical to carry along more than one fishing outfit. Usually it's a 7-foot casting rod with an 8-inch-long rear grip for leverage. On it is a free-spool, level-wind reel filled with 12-pound line. A spare spool of line is a must. My shoulder bag contains plastic boxes, each holding a specific type of lure, such as surface, deep divers, spinners, jigs, weedless spoons, and plastic worms with assorted sliding sinkers and hooks. A pair of long-nose pliers with a side-cutter is indispensable. And, of course, so are snacks like hard candies, dried fruit and nuts, sandwiches, and a small canteen of water. I find when the inner man is content, the outer man fishes better.

When you fish a shore, let the cover dictate the lure. In heavy brush use a weedless spoon; in scattered grass try a jig or plastic worm; and over shallow shoals or weedbeds offer a teasing topwater lure. For shelving drop-offs or deep runs work a spinner both shallow and deep. An in-line spinner is especially adaptable to casting in many cover types because of its compact weedlessness.

Get into the water whenever possible. A low silhouette and quiet approach will spook fewer fish than looming tall on shores and sending out harsh footfalls. Glide your feet along as if you were snowshoeing rather then plopping them down and transmitting detectable vibrations.

If you hook a hefty bass when you're wading in light pants, be careful not to force it to you too soon. Wear it down until you can lead it safely to hand. An energetic bass may run between your legs and hook you on your own lure. It's painful enough if just one leg gets hooked, but you're in a heap of trouble if your legs are hooked together. It has happened.

Learn to read what's underwater by observing the features of the land running into it. A rocky point disappearing into a lake usually continues below at the same angle. Ditto with a stairstep shore, so study these and fish accordingly.

Especially good hangouts are old fences, hedge rows, stump fields, drainage ditches, dark holes, and bridge abutments. Old river oxbows, small stream inflows, and dark ledges are bass habitat. A good way to read bottom is to nudge it with a heavy jig, both to feel contours and to judge depths.

Streams are much easier to interpret than a lake because eddies and slick water tell you where boulders and channels are hidden. Wade the shallow sides and fish the deep ones, watching ahead for slots and pockets where big bass might be holding.

And always, but always, scan the water ahead of you for feeding fish. When you spot telltale swirls, approach cautiously and lay a quiet cast beyond, not on, the spot. Then slowly reel the lure into the action area. Also watch for minnows skittering or fish-eating birds gathered at one hole. Where there are minnows, there are bass.

Yep, you'll learn to use all your senses when fishing afoot. But the best one is common sense. Take it in moderation, with a buddy along when possible; stay with it seasonally and keep notes on dates, times of day, payoff spots, and lures and methods used, and you will succeed.

You will become an unofficial member of a very exclusive group of bass specialists, the waders. It's a challenge. And man, you'll never taste better fish than those you've toted a few miles!

When wade-fishing, let the cover indicate the lure. If your approach is quiet, bass this size go for lures gently dropped along dense shore growth and reeds, as shown. Try to fish upstream so the current will carry sounds of your approach away from the bass, which are facing upstream.

22 Cold-Weather Bass: Tough but Big

Die-hard bass fishermen are those who hang in there when early-winter winds puff frigid blasts up their shirttails. Lesser anglers give it up. The die-hard "finatics" know that bass will come tougher, but if they work for them they'll come bigger. Success depends on know-how. The one factor they keep foremost in their minds is the amazing tolerance of bass for a wide spread of temperatures.

Put trout in bass habitat and they'll do poorly—even die—in 80- to 90-degree waters. Yet put bass in 40-degree trout water and they'll do just fine. Contrary to what some anglers believe, bass don't become sluggish in cold water; they just need less food as their metabolism slows, and they become harder to catch. Here are some cardinal points to keep in mind as you bundle up and go cold-weather bass fishing.

Think deep

Seek the deepest holes bordering some kind of structure—brush, weeds, rocks, old roadbeds, trestles, and channels. At this time of year, deep can mean 20 to 60 feet, depending on the lake.

Think BIG lures and s-l-o-w retrieves

Bigger bass go for bigger meals now, because it means more food to lay up winter fat. Instead of the usual 6-inch worm, go for 9- to 12-inchers. Use larger crankbaits with monster lips to drive them deep and keep them there. To get down quickly to the very deep levels that bass seek at this time of year, use heavy slab spoons. Their "slide-off" action when jigged is appropriate behavior in lower water temperatures.

Also try 1-ounce jigheads with 4- to 6-inch paddletail grub bodies. Jerk baits rigged on a jighead are good for deepwater probing, as are heavier tailspinner lures. Work these over deep shoals, off rocky points, and in the bottoms of old stream beds.

Work these lures two to three times deeper than you normally fish. When fishing vertically, swim the heavier lures in a large circle, stopping to jig them at intervals. Keep moving along deep shores, hoping to cross paths with bigger bass seeking comfort and food.

Deep cranking

It pays to change from summer tackle to a more practical rigging for winter fishing. The big-lip crankbaits touted to go 25 to 35 feet deep will do so, if you fish them correctly.

First, use a 7-foot rod. Your average summertime cast of 25 to 35 feet won't give a deep-diving plug enough room to reach the needed depths. But with the leverage of a 7-foot casting rod you can drive longer casts up to 50 and 60 feet. And remember, the lighter the line, the deeper the plug will run. Ten-pound test will be heavy enough to land even lunker bass, because they're now mostly in open water, not around snaggy cover.

Of course, there's always a chance you'll hook into a whopper wintertime bass that dives into bottom cover. To prepare for this, set your drag just above the breaking point of your 10-pound line. Then when a big bass runs into cover, give it line and keep following it as it moves out. Wait until it stops, then reel slack out of the line and maintain a firm pressure. Let the bass run around against rod pressure until it tires and can be led to you. Don't try horsing it in except as a last resort, when it absolutely refuses to come out of bottom cover.

If you still find you just can't get deep enough, here's a tip for driving a crankbait to its deepest level: kneel in the boat and shove the rod tip down into the water. For every foot you submerge the tip, you drive the plug that much deeper.

Ace in the hole

Here's how to get a plug to work on bottom, regardless of how deep that might be. Tie on a large slim minnow, and find a slide sinker

A sinker musses up the bottom sediment. A trailing lure appears to be a feeding minnow, an ideal target for cold-water bass.

heavy enough to make it sink. With a toothpick, peg the sinker about a foot above the lure, Carolina style.

Cast this into the deepest holes you can find and let it settle to the bottom. Then work it back very slowly, stopping intermittently to twitch it a long time in one spot. Do this all the way back to your rod tip; it's one of the deadliest ploys.

Latitudinal bass

Bass south of the freeze line, especially in Florida, remain relatively unaware of winter because the changes in water temperatures and habitat are so minor. Bass north of the freeze zone sense the continuing drops in water temperatures, and their bodies gradually adjust to the extremes. In the south, bass fishing goes on much the same as usual, except during the approach of cold fronts. When one of these descends suddenly, it has a drastic effect on bass. The bigger ones seem to disappear for two to three days, and no one catches them.

During the filming of *Bigmouth*, a prize-winning film by noted producer/photographer Glen Lau, one of these cold fronts moved in overnight. We knew from past experiences that larger bass wouldn't be around, so we prepared to settle for smaller ones.

But Lau's questing mind said biggies had to be somewhere, so he donned his scuba gear and began searching. After a long while, he returned with a big grin on his face and commented:

I found those big rascals. They were hiding in odd places, like deep in eel grass on the bottom, and way back under big cypress tree roots.

But here's a stumper. All those bigger bass seem distressed somehow, unable to function as usual. On the bottom they were bunched up and seemed to be leaning on each other. Under the big cypress trees they were resting on the roots.

I lifted one big bass away from her support and released her. She turned upside down, seeming to have no sense of equilibrium. So I returned her to her resting spot. The big question is, why does a cold front affect bigger bass this way?

Over the years, several theories have attempted to explain this. The most prevalent one related to the sudden drop in water temperature; even a few degrees could put the chill on bass. We blew that theory because we were fishing in Florida's Silver River at its source, Silver Springs, where 500 million gallons of water spew out every day at a constant year-round temperature of 72 degrees.

No one really knows why cold fronts affect big bass, but your Uncle Homer has a pet theory. We lived in Michigan for sixteen years, and almost every year during dog days a sudden cold front would hit Lake Michigan so hard that it bashed both east and west coasts with near–tidal waves. The cold air in that front had to dump its heavy air with tremendous pressure to do this. So, assuming that same sharp change in relative barometric pressure is suddenly exerted against southern bass, I believe this could affect bigger bass and stress them as described. Just one fisherman's theory, mind you.

So if you're fishing south of the freeze line during the winter when a cold front slams down, forget big bass. Go for the smaller ones with smaller lures—or go after panfish like bluegills, crappies, and catfish and have some finger-lickin' good cookouts!

Cold-weather bassing can chill you to the bone, unless you dress for it. From bottom to top, here is my choice of wear. Feet: lightweight cotton socks under a pair of insulated booties that absorb perspiration; lightweight insulated boots, 6-inch tops. Body: quilted long underwear; wool pants and shirt; knitted sweater; lightweight jacket and pants made of waterproof, breathable material. Hands: gloves of flexible, insulated material, with thumb cut out. Thus layered, you will contain body heat for early-morning fishing; as the day warms, one layer at a time can be shed for comfort.

23 Successful Trolling

Trolling is a gambler's way for finding fish on an unfamiliar body of water. It tips the odds in his favor because he can cover more water in the available time. But there's more to successful trolling than simply dragging lures behind a boat.

In the BS (Before Sonar) days of fishing, we trolled an unknown lake or stream to get an idea of depth, bottom cover, and contour. The feel of our bottom-bumping lures told us if they were engaging logs, brush, weeds, timber, boulders, gravel, etc. We kept sketches in a log book and referred to them when we returned to that body of water. Today, the process is much easier using a sonar unit, especially when combined with topographical maps, which point the way to the drop-offs, old channels, midlake humps, and other promising areas for trolling.

Trolling is effective for all gamefish, not just bass. Perch, white bass, crappies, pike, walleyes, trout, salmon, and striped bass and hybrids may all be taken by trolling. The tactics are the same, only the tackle is different.

For bass, you can use whatever rods and reels you already own, be they spinning, spincasting, or baitcasting. Favor a medium-action rod, which will set the hook better on a long line and help you boss big fish out of heavy cover.

For line, try one of the new fused braids in 40-pound test. It has the diameter of 12-pound mono, offering less water resistance and getting maximum action from diving-wiggling lures.

Part of successful trolling is choosing the best trolling lures and knowing their optimum trolling speeds. You determine this by holding a lure alongside the boat on a short line so you can observe its action. Start slowly and as you increase speed, notice when the lure has its best-balanced action. Then troll it at this pace.

Most boats will do for trolling, provided the outboard will throttle down to a purr that barely moves you along. For quieter trolling at far less expense, consider an electric trolling motor.

The best trolling lures are those that will cover all depths from surface to bottom, because bass hold at various levels depending on season, water temperature, clarity, atmospheric pressure, wind, and changing weather. Here are payoff lures in my trolling kit and ways to fish them.

Surface lures

These types of lures work best on days when surface waters are calm and bass are looking skyward for food. They include floating lures with either one or two spinners; weighted spinner lures with bucktail or plastic skirts and oversize spinner blades, which make them rise to the surface when speeded up; slim minnow lures with a small lip to keep them just below the surface at slow speeds; wobbling surface lures that create a commotion; crankbaits with big lips to make them run deep; and weedless types for weedy areas.

Choose lures that have good actions at very slow speeds. Troll them on or just below the surface, making commotions, even soft wakes, to get the attention of bass.

Medium-running lures

These lures have medium-size lips and are designed to run at 3- to 6-foot depths. Select sizes from ⅓ to ½ ounce in a range of natural patterns on flashing metallic backgrounds. Fine-tune each one to run on a true center and for superfast trolling when needed. Here's how.

Set your motor for a slow trolling speed, about 5 miles per hour. Keep a pair of pliers in your lap, and attach a lure to the line. Let out enough line to hold the lure alongside your boat and observe its action.

If it runs with an even beat on a centerline with no side dashes, speed it up to about 15 miles per hour. Say it runs to the left. Bend the line tie as you look the lure in the face, a tad to the right until it tracks on dead center. If it runs to the right, adjust the line tie to the left as needed. Properly tuned, your diving-wiggling lures should swim dead center at any trolling speed. However, some lures refuse to run on center no matter what you do to them. You can give these to beginners for practice lures.

Troll medium-running lures in, around, and over shore covers, first slowly, then extremely fast. Sometimes when bass are hanging tough, a lure that zips past at 12 to 15 miles per hour can stimulate them into striking, especially 1 to 3 pounders. The larger bass tend to hang out in greater depths, so let's go after them with deeper divers.

Deep-running lures

These are quickly recognized by their oversize lips, which make them dive to 10, 20, even 30 feet. And that's where you'll find the larger bass during extreme swings of water temperature, either very warm or very cold.

First you'll need to adjust each lure to run on a straight line, as outlined above. Head for the deeper drop-offs bordering steep banks, cliffs, ripraps, dams, channels, and old stream beds. Offer bass a variety of lure sizes, colors, depths, actions, and speeds.

As you troll, keep your eyes sweeping the entire area. Look for splashes from roving bass or for diving birds feeding on minnow schools. Stop trolling and work minnowlike lures ahead of such action.

It's important to know how much line you have out when a bass hits, so after you set the hook, mark the line just in front of the reel with a felt-tip marker. After removing the bass, pay out line to the marker and you'll know the lure is traveling at the same depth when you retrace the area.

When fishing with a buddy, a canny way to work out the pattern of the moment is for each to use lures of different depths, colors, actions, and sizes. As you troll, stay close to dark cover outlines and troll these in both directions to give each troller an equal chance. When making sharp U-turns, you can prevent tangled lures if the troller on the inside of the turn reels in his lure and then pays it out again upon returning to a straight line.

Also try wind trolling. When there's enough wind to carry the boat along, use a jig-grub lure heavy enough to permit working it vertically below your rod tip. Jig it just over bottom, and when you catch a bass, toss out a marker so you can return to the same spot. Remember, a skilled troller never needs to stop by the fish market on the way home!

24 Nuances of Night Bassing

W hen your favorite lakes go flatter than a flyswatter, when pet lures fail to allure, when you can't catch a single bass (or even a married one), do what canny fishermen do. Begin fishing when everyone else is quitting. In short, try night fishing.

These daytime doldrums occur mostly during hot summer months, especially on certain bodies of water. Typical are those that become exceptionally clear, enabling bass to see you from farther away, and those where heavy fishing pressure makes larger bass wary, hiding out in heavy cover when they detect fishermen sounds.

Here are some things to look for as you select night fishing spots: 1) shorelines with ample cover such as weeds, lily pads, roots, brush, and cattails that border deepening water; 2) lakes with a history of consistently good bass fishing; and 3) streams and ponds that can be fished from shore. And as you night-fish, keep a record of best catching hours and lures, water temperatures, and moon phases. These become invaluable in planning next year's night-bassing trips.

Before we discuss the best tactics for catching big, nocturnal-feeding bass, let's review the senses bass rely on in the dark so that we can tailor our appeal to them.

Of the five senses—sight, smell, taste, feel, and hearing—feel and hearing are the most important. We feel with our hands and skin and hear with our ears. Bass hear by feeling vibrations, such as those given off by wiggling lures or slithering worms, through neuromasts, the tiny nerve endings covering their sides. Through hollow bones and an air bladder they can hear the same sounds we hear, such as hooks rattling on metal hangers or noises from built-in rattling devices.

So for nighttime fishing, think vibrations and sharp sounds, and remember that bass don't need to see something to know it's there. Their sonar system is so sophisticated and sensitive that they can detect an unseen object's shape and speed and plot an interception course. And they can detect our presence just as easily, so total silence is called for.

Best lures

At night, you want lures that make sounds attractive to bass. These include lures with cupped faces that pop, chug, or burp; floating lures with one or more spinners that swish or splutter; slim minnows with small lips that make them swim or dive like an injured minnow; lipless floaters with no action except that imparted by the angler; and self-activated types that wobble or gurgle when reeled steadily.

Lures of these types produce best when the surface is calm and bass can hear and feel their vibrations at extreme distances. Work poppers slowly and quietly on calm nights, with long pauses between twitches. If it breezes up, work poppers with a little more noise.

You can work spinner-type lures the same way, but here's a neat trick for a special effect. Wrap enough lead wire around the shanks of each hook to cause the lure to sink slowly. Retrieved slowly, the spinners will muss up the water just below the surface and make a soft V that bass will come from surprising distances to attack.

Lipped lures

This family of crankbaits has varied lengths of lips to make them run from shallow to deep. Here are some retrieves to try. Cast, let it sit for a ten-count, twitch, twitch—and repeat the process at least a dozen times. Next, cast out, reel slowly for several turns of the reel handle, let it lie for a ten-count, and repeat all the way back. Also—and this will sound odd because it is—cast out and retrieve with quick half-turns of the reel handle, sort of "stumbling" the lure along.

Lipless floaters

This type of lure has no action of its own; animating it requires skill. Practice working these lures during daylight hours so you can see what's happening. Then you can envision it at night.

Cast out, let the lure lie until the shock waves subside, then point your rod tip in the direction of the lure. Now begins a cadence that starts with two short twitches of the rod tip followed by two quick turns of the reel handle: twitch-twitch, reel-reel, twitch-twitch, reel-reel—all the way back. This is "walking the dog." The lure will sashay, or swing its head back and forth, producing an action entirely different from that of any other surface lure. It's my favorite night charmer.

Self-activators

Lures like the Jitterbug and Crazy Crawler have built-in actions and waddle or paddle their way along with the angler's smallest movement. So do just that most of the time. Cast, and the instant the lure alights, begin a steady retrieve all the way back. Vary this occasionally with stop-and-go action, as if your lure is scared or confused. These noisy lures work quite well on choppy surfaces, also.

Alien surfusser

One of my best BIG-bass surface lures wasn't designed as a surface lure at all. It's the giant 12-inch worm, made of buoyant plastic, that's heavy enough to cast without additional weight. Use a curlytail design and rig it weedless with a 5/0 or 6/0 hook. Cast it into the worst of surface covers, where most lures would get ensnared, and reel it s-l-o-w-l-y and steadily along, stopping now and then as if to rest. The curlytail will flutter along behind this gargantuan worm, telegraphing a strong appeal to the nearest whopper bass. No other surface lure looks more natural or vulnerable.

Nighttime colors

One of the oldest beliefs is, "The blacker the night, the blacker the bait." Many old-timers swear by it, while others believe just the opposite. Only on bright, moonlit nights do they fish black—because it offers a contrasty silhouette against the lighter sky.

My personal experiences lean toward the latter group. When there is a little light in the water, I use light reflectors like white, yellow, and glittery colors. I'm convinced that when there is no light, there is no sight.

For fishing at night, color takes a backseat to sound, so I choose a variety of surface lures to find one that outcatches all others. This is part of the intrigue of night fishing: finding the key that opens those big locked jaws.

Another part of the charm of night fishing is to go with a bassin' buddy just as tetched about it as you are. Night fishing provides a relaxed atmosphere in which you take the time to swap yarns and try crazy tactics, and when one of them happens to work, you've caught a keeper memory.

Night fishing for bass is as peaceful as it comes; you begin when everyone else is quitting. You have the lake to yourselves and it's a great time for unwinding, retelling old fishing tales, sipping coffee when the night air cool, and listening to myriad night sounds. Catching bass is nice, yes, but it is incidental to the enjoyment of sensing the outdoors and the camaraderie of a bassin' buddy. When you return home you will never enjoy a deeper, more assuaging sleep. And when you awake, gone will be the job shackles and nerve wrinkles. Man, talk about an appetite!

25 How to Catch Bass Like a Pro

So you have a yen to fish like the pros and catch as many bass as they do. Well, you could, but chances are you won't. The reason is that a pro is compelled to master the regimen, but you aren't. You be the judge.

Here are some of the hurdles you'll need to master, learned from a dozen of the nation's leading pro bass fishermen with whom I've fished, including Roland Martin, Ricky Clunn, Hank Parker, Ken Cook, Cliff Craft, Bobby Murray, Larry Nixon, Tommy Martin, Ron Shearer, Bill Dance, Tom Mann, Guido Hibden, Larry Lazoen, Jimmy Houston, and Shaw Grigsby.

- **The challenge** of laying lures accurately and softly into as many spots as possible in a given period of time to catch the greatest poundage of bass, fishing against the nation's best pro-bass anglers

- **The skill** to approach bass hangouts quietly within 10 to 30 feet and be able to flip and pitch lures into teacup-size pockets

- **The discipline** to stand up all day on the bow deck, operating an electric motor with your foot or knee and forsaking your pet overhead cast in favor of flipping and pitching

I've kept score, and on average 50 percent of the pros' casts were flipping and 40 percent were pitching. This leaves only ten casts in a hundred for the overhead cast, which most anglers use 90 percent of the time. But there are good reasons the pros abandon the overhead cast. It's the least accurate of the three because it minimizes hand-eye coordination; with the overhead cast you can't see the lure until it's as least two-thirds of the way to the target. And because it's a much faster cast, it's more difficult to control and the lure alights with a harsher sound, which can spook wary bass. Finally, because overhead casts are longer, they use up valuable fishing time retrieving the lure, as compared with minimal retrieve time for flipping and pitching.

Flipping and pitching

Now, let's eyeball flipping and pitching in detail, beginning with flipping. First, do away with the swivel seat on your front boat deck because you'll need the room for maneuvering. Approach bass cover quietly and slowly, halting about 8 to 15 feet distant. Face the target, rod tip pointed overhead, and let the lure hang down about even with the rod butt. (When flipping, the spool doesn't turn on a level-wind reel.)

How to Flip
Face the target, 8 to 15 feet distant. Let the lure hang down even with the rod butt. With your free hand, grasp the line below the first guide and pull off about 6 feet of line from the reel.

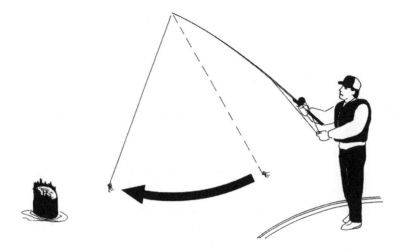

Raise and push the rod tip out to swing the lure gently over the objective.

Let excess line flow through your fingers, easing the lure onto the target. The reel spool does not revolve.

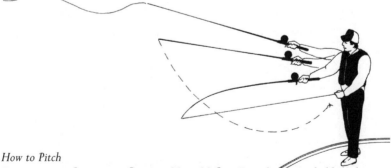

How to Pitch

For targets too far away to flip, say 20 to 30 feet. Face the target, hold the lure in your free hand and point the rod toward the target. Pull back on the lure to put a slight bend in the rod. Release the lure; rod flex will propel the lure onto the objective. The reel spool revolves to pay out enough line to drop the lure onto the target.

With the free hand, pull about 6 feet of line from the reel, raise and push the rod tip outward to gently swing the lure over the target like a pendulum, then lower the rod tip to ease the lure into the water, letting excess line flow through your fingers. The lure will slip under the surface, settling naturally to the bottom. Raise and lower the lure for about thirty seconds, then ease it out of the water and onto the next likely hangout.

As you can see, flipping is more accurate than overhead casting because your eye is on the lure from the moment it begins moving forward until it's lowered onto the target. And you'll hook and land more bass when flipping because the short line stretches less, allowing you to bury the barb more efficiently.

Pitching is a longer cast—up to 30 feet—for places you can't approach closely enough to flip and for very clear water where bass tend to be spooky. Here are the mechanics: Face the target, rod tip pointed overhead, the lure hanging down even with the rod handle. With your free hand, grasp the lure firmly, point the rod tip toward the target, and pull back on the lure to put a slight bend in the rod. Release the lure and let the rod tip propel it; the reel spool revolves to pay out enough line to ease the lure onto the objective. If it's done correctly, you can place lures into tiny pockets, deftly, accurately, and quietly. Another variation of pitching is to hold the rod parallel to the water instead of overhead, to make a flatter, perhaps quieter, cast.

Pro tackle

The major difference between a flipping rig and a pitching rig is the line. Flipping is done in all types of cover, especially brush, lily pads, roots, cattails, and branches, so the line needs to be strong and tough. The new multibraid lines with 40-pound test and 10-pound diameter are ideal for hauling lunkers from tough cover.

Pitching is used to present lures into cover edges, rifts, and open pockets. Since there's no need to horse bass out of dense cover, you can use lighter line, which casts more easily and can be used with lighter lures when needed.

A typical flipping rod is 6 to 7 feet long with a 3-inch foregrip and a 6- to 10-inch rear grip. The action is stiff to lend muscle for wrestling big bass from heavy hangouts. Pitching outfits vary depending on needs. For lighter lures in the ¼-ounce class, light-to-medium actions are used with varying tip flexes. Rear grips are 6 to 10 inches, with 3-inch fore-grips. Rod lengths vary from 5½ to 7½ feet. Pros shun casting rods with pistol-grip handles. They're tiring to use and lack the leverage for casting, hook setting, and hauling lunkers out of heavy cover.

Here's how pros rig for competition: Five to seven rigs are laid out, ready for action. Only one will be a spinning rig; the rest are casting outfits, because the constant line control by the thumb makes for more accurate pitching, softer lure presentation, better hook setting, and more control over hard-fighting fish. A spinning rig is necessary because it will do two things a baitcasting reel can't: cast lures lighter than ¼ ounce and bring in more line per turn of the handle when superfast retrieves are desired.

Retrieve ratios of baitcasting reels vary from 7:1 for superfast speeds to 4:1 for normal retrieves and greater fighting leverage. Lines are changed daily and vary from 6- to 15-pound test. Reels are checked and lubricated religiously.

Like most bass fishermen, the pros use an electric motor for moving the boat quietly along. But since the usual sharp-angled foot control is uncomfortable to use while one is standing up, most pros prefer a manual handle with an extension, steering either by hand or by knee.

Time and efficiency are valuable to a pro and both are served by having several outfits rigged and ready for action. These will range in rod actions and in lines from light to heavy; and each outfit will be rigged with a different type of lure for fishing top to bottom, in both weeds and open water.

Some of the newer radio-operated motors have a flat foot control that is quite comfortable to use. Pros don't feel that the sound of electric motors spooks bass, especially if run mostly at low speed.

Obviously, if you're flipping and pitching from the bow deck like the pros, your fishing buddy will have to do likewise from the rear deck. Working that close to cover, the overhead cast is impractical.

And remember, fishing from the rear deck and trying to find a spot where an adept front-deck caster hasn't already laid a lure is like trying to find a kernel of corn behind a hungry rooster. Swap off time on the front deck to share bass-catching opportunities.

Pro techniques

To help you fish like a bass pro, here are some of the techniques I've gleaned from fishing with many of the nation's best. One key question I asked each was, "What kind of spots do you seek to catch tournament-winning bass?" The prevailing answer: "Wherever a bass might be and no one else has laid a lure."

Ken Cook put it neatly: "I look for a good spot covered by an old spiderweb." All constantly look for havens good anglers might pass up because they appear impossible to reach. The pros have the skill to lay lures into such spots and the patience to work the lures as long as they take, because older bass are used to seeing lures hit and run away. A dallying lure can goad a big bass into attacking, so "easy does it" is a pro byword.

I have seen pros deliberately cast over a protruding branch and dance the lure on the water, using the limb for leverage. They lay lures in places so snaggy they're apt to lose a lure if a bass doesn't latch on. Now that's finesse!

They cast over, under, into, around, and behind obstacles to reach seemingly impossible places. They twitch, jiggle, swim, jerk, dangle, fast-and-slow crank, and animate lures in many ways to give bass something they may not have seen before.

Which lures dominate? For flipping, most are weedless for fishing heavy cover. Popular types are 4- and 6-inch Texas-rig worms, small leadhead jigs with soft plastic bodies or skirts, large weedless jigs with bulky crawfish or lizard bodies, and jig-and-pork combinations.

For pitching, the pros favor types that chug, spin, or buzz on the surface; crank and vibrator types that run from shallow to deep; plastic worms; jigs, weedless spoons, and in-line spinners; and slab spoons for deep jigging.

Tackle boxes are large with drawers crammed full of an infinite variety of lures, arranged by size, color, and design for reaching all manner of hangouts. The pros have all these lures cataloged in their minds along with countless fishing memories. Any combination could be the key to winning an important bass tournament.

And the pros have their mental concentration such that I've hesitated to ask questions. Once I was having a sandwich and asked Rick Clunn if I could fix him one. He replied, "No thanks, Uncle Homer, it might break my thought pattern. Maybe later."

Some pros can carry on a conversation and not lose concentration, but their minds are still keyed to the lure's feel—what it's touching, how it's capering, every iota of the retrieve. This kind of feel doesn't come easily, but there is a way for you to acquire this touch, even if you aren't able to fish as much as a pro.

Go to a swimming pool or a very clear pond with each of the favorite lures mentioned above. Cast each out and observe closely how it touches down, sinks, and reacts when twitched or reeled at various rates. This will give you a mental picture of what each lure is doing when you're animating it for bass.

The occasional angler will find it difficult to achieve the super accuracy of the pro. It takes thousands of hours of flipping and pitching lures until you can do it without thinking of each move. But if you have the desire, you can master these skills at home, in an hour or so each day. You need continuity to crease the memory track.

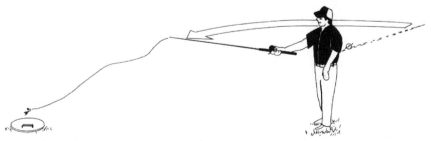

Home Practice
A low, flat, backhand cast at a garbage can lid at home will sharpen your hand-eye coordination for accuracy. And this low presentation gently eases the buzzer lure onto a target without spooking bass.

You'll find me practicing with a weedless lure in my yard, flipping and pitching into every nook and cranny. Neighbors think I'm peculiar. Well, I am, especially when it comes to bass fishing!

About wifely complaints

Many bass fishermen spend so much time—especially weekends—at their favorite sport that wives have a right to complain. But few wives see so little of their hubbies as those married to bass pros. How do they cope?

Jimmy Houston encouraged his wife, Chris, to enter women's bass-fishing tournaments. He taught her basic skills, then she developed her own ways of catching bass and became one of the Bass'n Gals Tournament's most consistent money winners.

A few wives attend tournaments and root for their hubbies. Others keep the home fires burning by taking care of business and the kids. Some were unable to cope and divorces resulted.

Larry Lazoen has a wife and two children, and I asked him how often he was home. He replied, "About three days during busy months." "Is your wife happy?" I asked. He said "About three days a month!"

Take your wife bass fishing; she might like it. Take her bouquets of wildflowers instead of bass. Give her a day that's all hers. Let her know how special she is—because she is, you know!

Tricks of the trade

The day I fished with him, B.A.S.S.-Classic winner Hank Parker won a tournament using an unusual tactic few other pros would attempt. A topographical map of the lake showed a dam on a small feeder stream at the back of a long, narrow bay. The entrance was blocked by floating logs deposited by rains and high water. Parker set his outboard in the tilt position so it would climb up and over each log encountered head on.

It took at least half an hour of valuable time literally to bulldoze his way to that small dam, where he knew flowing water would likely hold feeding bass. And because of the difficulty of reaching the spot, he knew few other pros would chance it. He caught three hefty bass there each day of the three-day tournament and won it!

Another tournament pro saw a bassy-looking bay but couldn't get to it because his boat was a tad too high to go under the low bridge across its entrance. He pulled the drain plug and loaded his boat with water until it sunk low enough to pass under the bridge. And he caught enough bass to make him the winner. How's that for ingenuity?

26 Hot Dam Fishing and Cruising Bass

B ass live in two main water worlds: still water and moving water. Nowhere is water more evidently on the move than below a dam. And it must be good fishing. Look down from any dam, and you'll almost always see elbow-to-elbow fishermen in the tailwaters, which are home to many species of fish—especially big bass.

As you look at them, you'll note that some anglers sit in one spot and hope fish will come to their lures. With fish on the move after mobile minnows, it does happen. But the wiser dam fishermen watch for movements that indicate feeding fish and head to the best points for reaching them. To make the long casts necessary to reach a feeding frenzy, they usually use 7- to 9-foot rods with big spinning reels and jigs and spoons weighing several ounces.

Still others fish from anchored or moving boats, where the waters aren't too swift. And where the shorelines permit, wading can be the deadliest of all approaches.

I have one special "keeper memory" of a dam-fishing article I wrote for *Sports Afield,* one I stumbled onto driving north of Little Rock, Arkansas. We were parked on Nimrod Dam, looking down at the fishermen below, and one man caught our attention.

He was in waders, chest-deep from shore and casting upstream. As we watched, he caught a good fish and added it to a stringer already heavy with fish. Now this will get any fisherman's attention, so we headed down the bank to get a better look at this canny angler.

As we arrived, he was adding another fish to his stringer, and we asked what he was catching. He grinned and showed us bass, white bass, crappies, catfish, bluegills, and walleyes, six sporting and tasty species. He was casting upstream with a heavy bobber; suspended below was a leadhead curlytail jig that the bobber activated as the current bounced it up and down. He adjusted the bobber up and down several feet to vary the depth and determine if the fish were holding at a certain level. We were impressed and returned later to share in the fun.

Since then I've become convinced that some of the most productive yet underfished waters around the nation are the moving-water streams below dams. My favorite way to fish them is in chest waders, using a baitcasting rig and a belly box holding lures selected especially for use in current: leadhead jigs with soft, curlytail bodies; in-line spinners; crankbaits; lipless crankbaits; slim minnows; buzzbaits; and slab spoons.

In fast currents, cast upstream with spinners, lipless crankbaits, and jigs. Ease them along until you feel the current begin to animate them, then keep them coming slowly and steadily over the bottom. In slower runs use lipless crankbaits, crankbaits, and slim minnows fished from top to bottom. In long, slow runs try buzzbaits in smaller sizes, and keep them buzzing, at times just below the surface.

Catching can be hot in the turbulent waters below a dam like this one, Nimrod Dam, in Arkansas. Minnows are the main diet, so the best lures are those that look and wiggle like shad or shiners. Casting bobbers add distance to casts and are needed to reach midstream holding spots.

In quiet backwaters use floater-divers—slim minnows and crankbaits. Work the deeper shores from top to bottom. These are also good spots for Texas-rigged plastic worms. Where eddy waters move upstream, try jigs and slab spoons fished deeply over bottom structures.

Some larger rivers are best fished from a boat, using a Danforth anchor to hold steadily on rocky and sandy bottoms. You'll soon learn to read the current flows that point out the deeper holes, behind-boulder eddies where bass hold when they're in a feeding mood, and undercut banks, especially where debris piles up.

One of the added bonuses of stream fishing is the abundance of wildlife. Keep alert for raccoons, foxes, squirrels, possums, and deer; hawks, owls, pheasants, grouse, quail, and other birds on the wing; and countless little critters in the water such as frogs, waterdogs, hellgrammites, leeches, minnows, crawfish—any one of which could be a clue to the lure you should be using. On many trips, nature's wonders caught by eye compensate for a lack of bass caught by hook and line!

BASS ON THE MOVE

In still water, bigger bass have two movement patterns to remember. One is probing shorelines to find food when it becomes scarce in their usual haunts. The other is cruising open waters and sometimes mysteriously stratifying in deep water for reasons unknown even to studious biologists.

These two patterns occur mainly before and after the spring spawning periods and during the late-fall feeding sprees as the bass put on body fat to survive the lean days ahead. Studies of radio-transmitter-equipped bass over many years have revealed some intriguing movement habits.

During the prespawn period, when waters begin warming and creating physiological changes, bigger females tend to bunch up and cruise together. On larger reservoirs this can encompass miles of travel for two main purposes. One is to feed before the upcoming rigors of spawning. The other is to seek out likely areas where male bass soon will begin fanning bottoms to create nesting sites.

These schools of roaming bass are believed to be made up of flushers and prowlers—a pecking order similar to that of many pack hunters seeking food. The smaller, more active bass are the flushers—forging ahead much like hunting dogs, busting in and out of shore cover to spook minnows and other food fishes into the open where the bigger bass crash into them.

So remember: If you're fishing along a cover line and catching numerous small bass, the whoppers could be holding just away from the cover in open water, waiting for baitfish flushed out by their confederates. Make it a habit to fire a few periodic casts into open water away from the shoreline covers.

After spawning, some bigger bass regroup to cruise the lake, covering many miles in larger bodies of water. Regularly, for some peculiar reason, they will stratify, or layer, in open water, far away from shore cover, sometimes over midlake structure at depths from 10 to 50 feet. At times it's near the thermocline, but usually temperature and oxygen have nothing to do with it.

Here are two ways to find suspended bass. First, examine topographic maps to pinpoint these deeper, offshore areas. Try fishing these with deep-diving lures, plastic worms, slab spoons, jigs, and spinners, at all depths.

If there is no action, try wind drifting or trolling over and around these spots at 10 to 50 feet. Once you catch bass at such a spot, triangulate it so you can return, and log it in your notebook. These holes can pay off again and again in future trips.

27 Seven Ways to Land Big Bass

L anding a bass is a fairly simple maneuver for an experienced angler—if it's an ordinary bass. But when it's the biggest bass of your lifetime, it's a different kettle of fish. You want to be certain you do it the safest way, and below you'll find seven ways tailored to different circumstances.

With any of them, the important thing to remember is not to try landing a giant bass until you're sure it's ready. This means playing it to the point when it's tired enough to be led easily to hand. At this point, carefully observe how the bass is hooked. If you're using a plastic worm or other single-hook lure, any of the seven methods will work, because the single hook usually poses no danger in handling. Most of the time it will be inside the bass's mouth.

However, if you're using a lure with two or more treble hooks and if one or more hooks are exposed outside the bass's jaw, you must choose the method that best fits the situation. And situations vary depending on whether you're in a boat or on shore.

Landing net

For less-experienced fishermen, a net is the best way to land that big bass. It's important to choose a landing net large enough to enclose easily the biggest bass you hope to catch. Never try to land a bass too big for the net; it could tangle hooks in the mesh and tear free. Choose another option.

But if you're sure the net is large enough and the bass is sufficiently pooped to be easily led, do just that. With about 4 feet of line off the rod

Photograph by Glen Lau.

tip, lead the bass away from the net while you quietly slide it into the water. This way the bass won't see the net enter the water and make a dash for freedom.

Hold the handle in your free hand and lower it into the water with a sweeping motion to open the mesh bag fully. Lead the bass until it's centered over the middle of the net, then quickly lift the net to enclose the bass.

Be certain the net is large enough to enclose the biggest bass you hope to catch.

Jaw grip

This is probably the most popular and the surest method, the one used by most experienced bass fishermen. It's popular because when aptly done, it paralyzes a bass, making it both safe and easy to land. However, there are some pointers to remember before using it.

Never reach for a bass's jaw with your bare hand if any treble hooks are hanging outside the jaw. One powerful shake of its head and *you* could be caught instead of the bass. This is a painful situation, especially if you're alone, so choose one of the other options below.

There is a right and a wrong way to grip a bass's lower jaw. Grab only the jawbone and a big bass will flop around and lacerate your thumb. The right way is to lay your thumb well over the center of the lower jawbone, curl your forefinger under the jaw, and grip tightly as you push upward on the tongue.

Pushing up on the tongue exerts pressure on the bass's central nervous system and paralyzes it. You can feel it go limp, incapable of any movement, except for minor twitches of the fins. Now you can safely hold the bass while you extract the hooks.

Gill press

This method should be used after you decide menacing hooks make the jaw grip risky. Span the bass's head with your hand, placing your thumb on one gill plate and fingers over the other. Apply gentle pressure and land the bass.

This is the surest way to land that special monster bass. Don't let it thrash around on top where it can tear loose. Instead, play it out until you can lead it to you easily, underwater. Place your thumb over the center of the lower jaw, cup your forefinger under the jaw, and push up on the tongue. This puts pressure on the central nervous system and paralyzes the bass. One word of caution: If a treble-hook lure is in the bass's lips, beware. A thrashing bass can bury a hook in your hand. Use the belly lift.

By spanning the head with your thumb on one side and fingers on the other, and by squeezing to apply pressure on the gills, the bass is paralyzed for handling.

The pressure on the gills temporarily paralyzes the bass, and it will hang motionless while you land it. Once you have it in hand, you can safely grip the lower jaw and remove the hooks.

Belly lift

When the bass is too big to span the head with your hand and compress the gills, use this method. Slowly ease your hand under the bass to cradle it in your cupped fingers, just ahead of the anus. Lift, letting the weight of the bass press against upward pressure from your fingers. This presses against the bass's central nervous system and paralyzes it. When you feel it go limp, lift it from the water and use the jaw grip to maintain the paralysis so you can safely remove the hooks.

Hoist

This is the method professional bass fishermen use, because it's the quickest way to get a bass into the boat. Get the bass coming toward you, then use the rod as a derrick to hoist it aboard. Many bassin' men don't use this method on big bass because the pressure can tear them loose. Just be certain your line is strong enough if this is your only option.

Cradle the bass in your hand and press up with your fingers on the soft belly area; pressure on the central nervous system will immobilize the bass.

Gill slot

If you catch a truly huge bass and you have no net or one too small, and you're too far from shore in a boat to try beaching it (see below), try this method. Play the bass until it's subdued and doesn't jerk when you touch it. Lead the bass alongside, lift with your rod tip until the bass's

The quickest and easiest way to land most bass. Play the bass until it's docile, bring it toward you, then hoist it aboard in one continuous motion.

Insert your forefinger into the gill slot in the center of the lower jaw, grip tightly, and lift.

head is out of water, then ease your forefinger into the gill slot under the chin. At the same instant, grip over the bass's jaw with your thumb and press it against your forefinger. There is no more secure grip than this on a big bass.

Beaching

If you've played out a monster bass and decided that the other six methods are too iffy, head your boat for the nearest shallow shore. Step ashore, and when the bass is docile, quickly drag it onto the beach.

Releasing bass

All the methods above are for landing *big* bass. We need to discuss the best way to handle the majority of bass we catch, those in the smaller sizes—from juveniles to "couple-pounders." Most bass fishermen release these to live on and delight other anglers. This is best done by not touching the bass with your bare hands. The amino acids on your hand are so strong that they can remove the protective mucus on the bass's body and leave the door open to an often-fatal fungus growth.

My customary method is to assess the position of the hook that's holding the bass. Most of the time, if you'll suspend the bass from the line and grip the hook shank with a pair of long-nose pliers, you can shake the bass free without touching it.

If you find it is necessary to hold the bass with one hand while extricating hooks with the other, wear a glove on the gripping hand to protect the bass from contamination. If you'd rather not mess with a glove, then do as some conscientious bass anglers do: Take along a zipper bag of baking soda, which is a good acid neutralizer. Wet your gripping hand and dip it in the soda before handling the bass.

Well, happy landings, and when you lose a giant bass, just remember: There are times when it's good for the bass to win. This ensures more giant bass in your tomorrows.

Go ashore, and when the bass is tired enough to be led, bring it toward you and beach it.

28 A Safe and Easy Way to Remove a Fish Hook

It happens to all of us sooner or later—a fish hook is painfully imbedded in you or your companion. So why not be prepared?

Here's a removal method that's remarkably easy to do and painless to boot. A cherished fishing buddy, Bob Steber, veteran outdoor columnist of the *Nashville Tennessean*, showed me this method. Over the years I have used it to remove five hooks, each leaving the hookee both pleased and pain free.

During one, a doctor happened to be present and watched the proceedings attentively. After I finished, he said that it was "a remarkably simple and efficient method. And I can assure you of one thing. I would have used a scalpel to cut it out and there would have been considerable pain both during and after the operation. I plan to use this method in the future."

First, a couple of observations. The simplest way to remove a fish hook imbedded past the barb is to push it on through, cut off the barb, and back out the hook shank. But light wire hooks that bend or a point imbedded against a bone can make this impossible.

If the hook is imbedded around the eye or close to an obvious blood vessel, get the victim to a doctor as soon as possible. But if a hook is imbedded in the hand, arm, leg, or scalp, where it can't be pushed through, then use this time-proven method.

Study the instructions carefully. And to really hone your skill, practice with a piece of line, a fish hook, and a potato. It could keep a fishing trip from turning into a bad memory and save a companion a lot of pain.

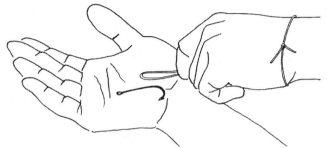

Easy Steps for Hook Removal
Line strength must approximate 20-pound test, or double a 10-pound line. Make a
12-inch loop, place it around the back of your hand, bring the eye of the loop
between your thumb and forefinger. If the hook is on a lure, disengage it.

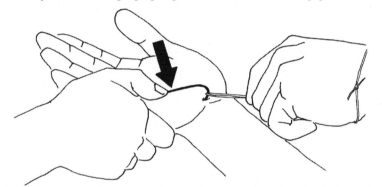

Place the loop over the eye of the hook and center it on the hook bend. Immobilize
the hand, or the part of the body where the hook is embedded, so it can't move. Apply
pressure downward and back on hook eye as you yank sharply on the loop.

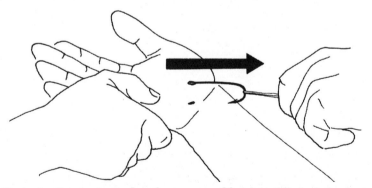

The hook will instantly pop free of a tiny piece of flesh behind the barb, leaving only
a minute hole in the flesh. Apply Bacitracin, or another antiseptic, and an adhesive
bandage. There should be a little immediate pain and no after pain.

It's a good idea to make a copy of this procedure and take it fishing with you—just in case.

Special note: Should you be fishing alone and get a hook imbedded where you can't use both hands to remove it, like in the back of one hand, do this: Anchor the loop around an oarlock, limb, or anything solid. Place the other end of the loop around the hook as illustrated, and jerk the impaled member in the opposite direction.

29 Bass Fishermen: North Versus South

I s there a difference between northern and southern bass fishermen? No, not *a* difference. I've seen *many* differences in over a half century of fishing for bass both above and below the Mason-Dixon Line.

It would be easy to refer to northerners as Yankees and southerners as rebels, but it wouldn't be prudent. I'd be certain to get letters asking, "How come you capitalized 'yankees' and put a little letter in 'rebels'? Note my small *y*." And if I replied that Webster's dictionary lists it that way, I could expect a return letter stating that "all the damned Websters I ever knew were Damnyankees. Note my big *D*!"

So let's just say northern bassers and southern bassers, and get on with the differences I've observed. First off, there's the pronunciation of the fish's name. In the midnorth its *baass*; in the northeast, *bahss*. In parts of the south it's *bay-ess*. But in most areas America's most popular game-fish is just plain *bass*.

One of the major differences, of course, is the fishing season. Northerners have to settle for a shorter go at bass because the water hardens on them until it's only good for skating and cooling bourbon. Many count time until next bass season by ice fishing through the long winter.

But I'll tell you what: Southern bass fishermen have it made— twelve full months of enjoying their favorite fish. While it does get cold, with the wind-chill factor down around zero at times, the southern boys tough it out with the help of a local device called a magnum hand-warmer. It's an old minnow bucket with two inches of gravel on the bottom and glowing charcoal on top. Shove a pair of frigid hands into one of these and you get instant relief.

At times, on big impoundments, southerners will be fishing over 75-foot bottoms, very deeply and s-l-o-w-l-y. How slowly? Well, I once asked this question of a bassin' pal in "Tinnissee," and he replied: "See that snail down there on that ledge? Jist about that fast, hear?" We were fishing a jig and pork frog.

There's a yarn about one of these hill-clan southerners who was bass fishin' on a bone-chilling morning. He had prepared for it by taking along a jug of moonshine to counteract the shivers. He counteracted a few times and got to feeling warm all over and humming to himself. Then he looked into the minnow bucket and got to feeling sorry for them, because all they had to drink was water.

So he sprinkled a generous spurt of moonshine into the minnow bucket, smiled at how active they'd suddenly become, hooked a big one through the tail, and pitched it overboard. His bobber immediately swooshed out of sight; he hauled back on his pole and brought in an 8-pound bass. And that minnow had a death grip on the bass's throat.

In addition to tall tales like this, bass fishermen on both sides of "the line" also share ways to combat foul weather. While northerners do have a rainy season, it's mostly confined to spring, while southerners put up with rain all year. That's why I see mostly rubber boots in the South: northerners' leather boots can get mighty soggy down there.

Bass boats vary a lot, too. Up North they tend to be much larger, with big engines for making longer runs. And while you do see similarly equipped boats in the South, there are a lot more "good ol' boy" boats down there. Take a johnboat, for instance. To northerners this could mean a boat equipped with a potty for little kids and old men with TB (tiny bladder).

But to southerners, a johnboat is a lightweight portable craft squared off at both ends and propelled by a sculling paddle. It's used on small lakes, ponds, and river backwaters, where big boats equipped with heavy engines are impractical.

Southern bass fishermen have access to a lot more small lakes and ponds, on private lands and in national forests, where bigger boats just aren't practical, especially when you need to drag them to the water rather than launch from a paved ramp.

Bass fishing itself, especially methodology, has a number of differences. Take bass cover, for instance. Northern bass are found mostly around shore cover such as lily pads, weeds, brush, fallen timber, private docks, rock piles, etc. Likewise in the South, but down there bass are also found more in offshore cover such as midlake weedbeds, shoals, reefs, and deep holes marked by rags on three bushes to triangulate them.

Stream fishing is sharply different, too. Up North, rivers and streams tend to be larger and swifter and can be risky for boats that aren't large and rugged enough to take fast-water rapids and brushes with the occasional boulder. Currents flow so fast that it's necessary to anchor much of the time in order to fish banks or holes properly.

Southern rivers and streams are much like the folks who fish them. Instead of rushing pell-mell they just sort of mosey along at a leisurely pace, which is ideal for working lures, seldom needing to anchor in order to fish banks and holes.

Then there are the signs anglers look for to tell them when to go bass fishing. Many of my northern buddies believe in solunar tables, barometers, water-temperature changes, animal activity, and other natural phenomena.

Of course one of the best indicators of when to go fishing is when the ice melts. I've watched some overeager northerners with an overdose of cabin fever drag their boats over the ice to reach a patch of open water in the center of the lake. Never mind the hazard of getting the boat back onto the ice when the cabin fever cools. Being first to fight those bass each year is what counts.

Southern bass fishermen have another indicator that prods them into action each spring. They eagle-eye the dogwood trees. When the sun has warmed the ground enough for the dogwood blossoms to burst forth in their pink-and-white glory, they know it's also warmed the waters enough to set in motion the chemistry that compels monster bass to begin their lovemaking rituals in the shallows. And it's amazing how accurate this natural yardstick is.

And speaking of signs that indicate the best time for bass fishing, one of my colorful southern buddies told me about his infallible indicator: "I've tried all sorts of gadgets to tell me when to go bass fishin'. You name it, I've tried it. And I've found only one gadget that never fails to tell me exactly when to go. She weighs one-hundred-sixteen pounds and I married her 22 years ago!"

Bass-fishing tackle, including rods, reels, and lines, is much the same in both areas. Lures vary little as well. The popular bass catchers are surface chuggers and spinners, crankbaits with big lips to take them down sharply, lipless lures with rattles to sound off in dingy water, and overhead spinners for flash and flutter. Weedless spoons are used by both, but I believe more often by southern fishermen because of the heavier cover.

There is one big puzzler, however, and that's with the best bass catcher of all, the plastic worm. In the South, an estimated 50 percent of all bass fall for this nightcrawler replica. But in the North, the worm is far less catching. I've quizzed many topflight bass fishermen about why this should be, and their responses indicate that they're puzzled, too. Here are some of their answers.

"I think it's because of a difference in the diets of bass. I believe we have more waterdogs, leeches, eels, snakes, and other slinky critters down South," replied one southerner.

A northerner said: "I believe it's a whole different ball game up North because we have more weeds on our lake bottoms. It's a whole lot easier to work crankbaits and spinners over heavy weeds than to drag a weighted worm through them."

Another southerner said: "I just don't think Yankee fishermen have the patience to work a plastic worm slowly enough to catch bass. They're more used to banging out a plug and hurrying it back. Northerners always seem to be in a bigger hurry, even when they're fishing."

Well, I know some good southern worm fishermen whose jobs relocated them up North. I asked them the same question and one replied: "I wish I knew. I've tried hard, and these northern bass just won't eat plastic worms."

Another said: "I've been checking stomachs in lots of northern bass and have yet to find a worm, snake, or eel. I don't believe they recognize a plastic worm as something edible. Oh, I catch a few bass on them but only because I fish plastic worms far more than I should; I'm just too hardheaded to quit."

Well, I've fished the plastic worm in both climes, and up North I've caught twice as many bass on surface lures and crankbaits as I have on plastic worms. Frankly, I don't know why this should be.

Logic tells me that a bass, wherever it lives, doesn't take a plastic worm just because it's a dead ringer for a nightcrawler. These squirmy critters live in soil, not water. And I see no resemblance to the way a fisherman animates a plastic worm and the way an eel or leech swims along.

So I just accept the fact that northern bass simply don't go for plastic worms as do southern bass. But what the heck. How many northerners go for mushy grits and salty country ham? Differences make life interesting.

Another difference I've noticed is the way northern and southern bass fishermen look at age-old superstitions. While I was living in Michigan, a bass buddy pointed out to me the uselessness of going bass fishing when cattle are lying down. The best time, he said, is when cattle are up and around, eating and moving. He said he had kept track of this for years and had never had it fail.

I moved to Arkansas and latched onto a farmer chum also hooked on bass. We were sipping coffee on his back porch one spring morning before taking off for Beaver Lake. I noticed his milk cow was lying down and asked him what he thought about this old superstition.

He replied: "Yup, 'at's what my pappy taught me, too. And I watch ol' Betsy out there when I git ready to go bass fishin'. Iff'n she's on her feet and moving around, fine. Iff'n she ain't, well, jist afore I take off, I boot her in the butt to make sure the sign is right, then I go."

Which reminds me of another difference between northern and southern bass fishermen. In Ohio, where I was reared, Buckeye fishermen called them bass. In Georgia and Alabama I've been told in no uncertain terms that they're green trout. It's been thataway for umpteen years and no visiting yankee (note the small *y*) writer is going to change it.

Speaking of differences in lingo, one morning I was sitting on a boat dock waiting for an Alabama bassin' buddy to arrive. Two southern bass fisherman got out of their pickups, shook hands, and howdied each other. Here's the conversation I overheard.

"Jeetjet?"
"Nohowbowjoo?"
"Nope-avent, squeet."

Translation:

"Have you eaten yet?"
"No, how about you?"
"Nope, I haven't, let's go eat."

And finally, there's the way bass are eaten. Up North I notice a tendency to keep the larger bass for baking or filleting. One big bass goes farther than several smaller ones. Down South they tend to release bigger bass, in part so they can return to the business of raising more bass for tomorrow and also because big bass tend to have a strong flavor—bass between 1 and 2 pounds are better eating.

Which reminds me. When Childbride and I moved south, I thought it would be nice to mention it in one of my monthly magazine columns. So I began by announcing, "I done joined the South!" I got a letter from a Yankee reader (note the big *Y*) that read: "Damned good riddance . . . and don't think you will be missed!"

Yep, there always have been and hopefully always will be many differences between southern and northern bass fishermen. These make even stronger the common bond: They'll both drive hours to enjoy an occasional bass rather than minutes to catch a bunch of any other sporting species!

Wisconsin bass fisherman enjoy their sport year-round. These bass were caught in the Mississippi River in the late fall. Many prefer taking bass in the fall fishing because the flavor is milder due to the bass's limited diet. Some fish from heated shanties while others dress for frigid weather and spud their holes in the wide-open space.

30 The Ethics of Bed Fishing for Bass

S everal years back, when I noticed a growing number of fishermen trying to catch trophy bass by going after them on the beds, I asked dozens of bass fishermen for their opinions on this practice. The results of this survey should interest every serious bass angler.

As with most issues, there are two sides to the bed-fishing controversy, and each side has capable spokesmen. Many respondents were adamantly against it:

- "It's like ground-swatting quail or potshotting ducks. A true sportsman will have no part of it."

- "Well, I guess a guy who has no qualms about catching bedding bass wouldn't think twice about shooting a doe nursing a fawn."

- "I don't fish during the spawning season, never have, never will. Big bass don't mean that much to me. I catch bass to eat, not show off."

- "When I was younger we used to catch big sows off the bed, up to 15 pounds. But they're scarcer now and need protection."

- "To me bass fishing is the ultimate challenge of angling skill. Bed fishing is no challenge because it requires no skill, just persistence."

- "I don't think any creature should be harassed while mating."

But there's always another side of the coin, as seen in these quotes:

- "More trophy bass die of old age than are caught by fishermen, so why not bed-fish for them?"

- "Biologists tell us you can't fish out a large lake and that once a bed is vacated, more bass move in. And since there are far more bass beds than bass, why not?"

- "Big bass are old bass and less than 10 percent of their eggs will be fertile, and that's what most bed fishermen are after, big bass."

- "Why not? You can't catch them after summer and weeds take over a lake."

Note than many referred to "big bass," "trophy bass," or "old bass." This is important. In fact, I believe it spotlights the central point of this controversy. Bedding time is the only period of the year when big bass can be had with certainty.

Two bass spawning. Photograph by Glen Lau.

The bed-fishing specialist locates a number of bass beds and visits each several times until the big female appears—and nearly 90 percent of bass over 6 pounds are estimated to be females. She is harassed with both artificial and live baits until she grabs one defensively and is hooked. She doesn't take a lure from hunger, but from a need to protect her brood from this invasive menace.

Anglers seek these big bass for mounting, publicity, or conversation. Others are after a world-record bass with its promise of fame and fortune. And some guides charge $500, guaranteeing a 10-pound bass or no pay. One I met went twenty-four straight trips during spawning season before he missed taking a 10-pounder.

What happens to smaller bass caught off a nest and released? I asked this question of biologists who had studied the matter and they replied: "A female rarely returns, but the smaller male does most of the time. However, when neither returns because of harassment, count that hatch of bass lost."

Then there's the point that old female bass produce mostly infertile eggs, possibly as high as 90 percent. To learn the facts I sought out Doug Hannon, ESPN's "Bass Professor" and a specialist who has made in-depth studies of trophy bass. His reply:

> I know what biologists say about giant females being low in fertility, but there is one important factor favoring the protection of these trophies. There is a great possibility they are the gene pool for other giant bass.
>
> Most biologists agree that a bass is more likely to grow to mammoth size if it comes from a giant bass. Consider that probably less than one in 6,000 bass eggs lives to reach maturity, say 1½ pounds. Of 2,000 bass that reach maturity, only one reaches 10 pounds. That's why I return all bass I catch, especially the large ones that have a thousand times more chance of becoming a world record than progeny from a two-pounder.

How does Uncle Homer feel about bed fishing for bass? Well, I haven't killed a bass for my own needs in more than twenty-five years. I fillet smaller ones for old fish-loving friends who are unable to catch their own. All other bass, especially bedding bass, I return at once with minimal handling. If I accidentally catch a bedding bass, I release it at once at the nest site. By using artificial lures I rarely harm the fish, and I can live with this.

My observations and gut instincts tell me that if enough specialists bed-fish for bass, especially during peak spawning periods, the quality of bass in any lake will suffer. And I don't care for the practice of some guides targeting spawning fish for money.

As I look at the future of bass fishing, one thing appears certain: If water quality keeps deteriorating around our nation and if bass-fishing pressure continues increasing to the point when the average size falls off sharply in any lake, then we'll see widespread controls on sizes, limits, and seasons to protect the species.

And even though some biologists say such restrictions won't increase the catching of bass, I would welcome them. I believe it's high time we begin to show more concern for the welfare of our most popular gamefish and less for those who make money from it.

31 Bass-Fishing Tournaments: Good or Bad?

Bass tournaments have become big business across America, with thousands of such events held each year. But the question often arises, "Are they good or bad for the overall sport?"

How big have bass tournaments become? Across the country each week there are thousands of local bass-club tourneys with minor prizes and hundreds of interclub competitions with larger payoffs. Then there are four or more national "circuits" bankrolled by sponsors who profit from products sold to bass fishermen. The payoffs for these tourneys are big enough to provide upwards of fifty pro bass fishermen with a good full-time living.

The titan among tournament holders is the Bass Anglers Sportsman Society, founded by Ray Scott in 1967, when its initial tournament was held on Beaver Lake, Arkansas. I gave the benediction at the awards banquet, and at Scott's request counseled him on the pitfalls to be avoided if a national effort were to be successful.

Successful? Today the Bass Anglers Sportsman Society stages an average of fifteen tournaments each year, on both lakes and rivers, with payoff totals reaching into the millions of dollars. Entry fees for each event run from hundreds into thousands of dollars, and the prizes are lucrative indeed.

The top thirty money winners meet in an expense-paid annual tournament called The Classic. Upwards of 20,000 fans attend the three-day competition to cheer on their favorites, and more than one hundred national press-corps members attend the final award ceremonies, leaving no doubt that this is a class event.

The champion of champions takes home $50,000 in winnings and has a good chance at an additional million bucks in sponsorships, seminars, bass articles, TV appearances, and other commercial functions over future years.

B.A.S.S., as it's known, has grown into a very successful conglomerate. In addition to the tournament circuit, it publishes several magazines, including *Bassmaster, Southern Outdoors, Southern Saltwater, B.A.S.S. Times, Fishing Tackle Retailer,* and a national TV show, *Bassmasters.*

Scott sold his interest in recent years and now is president emeritus. Helen Sevier is the CEO and is carrying on the well-established traditions very capably. This all sounds very good for B.A.S.S., but what about the rest of us? Are thousands of bass tournaments "raping our lakes," as some resentful bass fishermen charge?

In the beginning, I had serious doubts about the impact of such large catches by all these skilled anglers. But through interviewing many state fish-and-game personnel who have policed tournaments, through personal observations of how the bass were handled before and after weigh-ins, and through establishing good friendships with dozens of the contestants, I no longer worry about the "raping" charge. Tagged bass showed a survival rate in the 95-percent-plus range, and I feel this reveals a genuine concern on the part of tournament anglers for proper release techniques and the preservation of the resource.

Some bass fishermen may hate the thought of tournament fishing, but I see more benefits than detriments. First, there are the people who make a full-time living from tournaments. In the beginning there was some rowdy conduct from a couple of participants. Scott refunded their entry fees and barred them from all future tournaments. End of rowdy conduct.

Those I know personally and call friend are mostly family men and gentlemen, a credit to the sport of bass fishing. They give their all in efforts to win and yet take time to put something of themselves back into the sport.

They give interviews to the outdoor press and are generous in revealing their winning methods or perhaps some unusual presentation that helped them capture a tournament. I have seen these same champions show empathy for a competitor who had a blank day by sharing with him a couple of their "honey holes" so he could get back in the race.

From tournament competitors have come not only new and better ways to find and catch bass but also many improvements in rods, reels, lines, boats, motors, and accessories. No one uses these harder nor is more aware of things that need improving, which is one reason so many serve as industry consultants.

Yes, I can understand a bass fisherman who goes fishing on "Lunker Lake" every weekend resenting the intrusion of professionals into his domain. I also know of some good bass fishermen who closely observe these sharp pros, who are uncanny at quickly ferreting out all the places bass should be. After the tournament, the observant resident bass fisherman has learned several new bass hangouts.

What's the future of tournament fishing? That largely depends on what happens to the quality of the water and bass habitat. Wherever either is allowed to degrade, bass populations decline. When this happens, state fishery departments usually respond with restrictions, such as a "slot limit" of 12 to 18 inches, for example. Only bass outside the slot can be kept; those inside must be returned because the larger bass are viable spawners and the smaller bass are fertile males.

It's up to us to be concerned enough to follow the lead of some bass fishermen, who form clubs (more than 2,500 now exist across the country) that study the needs of local areas and pressure state conservation offices to address the solutions.

Bass tournaments shine a spotlight on the quality of bass fishing in a chosen lake. When these experts can't catch an impressive total of bass, they just aren't there for the catching. Yes, I believe if we add up all the "pluses and minuses" of tournament fishing, the pluses will dominate. B.A.S.S., through its large membership, stays in constant contact with the powers that be in Washington and exerts pressure to correct any water or habitat deterioration they see.

To become a member of B.A.S.S. and receive its monthly mailings, which will keep you informed on the latest in bass-club activities and on fishing methods of the pros, and enable you to holler for help if there's a bass crisis in your area, write Bass Anglers Sportsman Society, 5845 Carmichael Road, Montgomery, AL 36117.

32 A Look at Bass Over the Years

Just another bass.

That's all I saw for nearly a half century as I caught thousands of keeper-size bass and tossed back undersize ones.

It was an ego kick. From the outset I fished arduously from dawn to dark and beyond. I was compelled to catch more bass, to build my image as an expert. Then my compulsion changed from quantity to quality. I pursued only trophy bass, using larger lures in deeper hideouts.

And I dogged them with a vengeance—almost to the point of addiction. We moved to central Florida, one of the prime factors being that it was the heartland of the world's largest bass.

Up to this point I had never mounted a trophy bass. Then I saw a mounting that impressed me—eight bass, each over 6 pounds, mounted on a stringer, as if they'd just been lifted from the water. I determined to have eight bass so mounted, each over 10 pounds, on my office wall. Something to gaze at and recall memories of battles won and lost over a lifetime. An ego kick to impress fellow bass anglers with my know-how at outwitting those wise old behemoths.

I vowed to catch my eight trophies on artificial lures, shunning the lesser challenge of using live shiners. Here would be proof of a lifetime spent fine-tuning angling skills. Yep, such a boggling stringer of bass would say it with gusto!

In just one month I caught two over 11 pounds and three over *10* pounds from a remote lake where I stumbled into a pocket of larger bass.

Homer Circle, circa 1980.

I worked out a deadly pattern, using giant plastic waterdogs, releasing dozens of bass in the 5- to 9-pound range. I told the taxidermist to keep the five trophies in the freezer until I brought the other three; then he could mount them.

But then something got in the way. I was asked to be the bass fisherman in a special documentary film about the world of bass, called *Bigmouth*. It took fourteen months of concentrated effort and study, living daily with largemouth bass and learning much about their lifestyle I had not previously known. (Still highly acclaimed as the most informative of all bass films, *Bigmouth* is available for $19.95 from Glen Lau Productions, 5640 SW Sixth Pl., Unit 400,

Through the eyes of the young men on the underwater cameras, who lived daily with bass, I learned more about bass than in all my previous forty-five years as a fisherman. The film became a classic—and a turning point in my philosophy.

During one session of filming striking, leaping bass, some in the 8-pound class, the director, Glen Lau, said seriously: "We'll never *throw* back a bass. Let's handle each one gently, and be certain it is not in shock before we release it. These are magnificent creatures and deserve both respect and compassion. We need to use them, but let's never abuse them."

Had this come from an ordinary film director, I doubt that it would have meant much to me. But Lau had been one of the nation's most successful bass-fishing guides, a Lake Erie legend who had caught and helped catch tons of fish. Such an empathetic assessment from this man touched off an intense desire in me to know everything possible about this creature, which suddenly had become more than just another conquest.

During filming I delved into the study of bass with even more zeal than I had exerted to catch them. I reported these findings in two special features called "The Underwater World of the Bass," which appeared in *Sports Afield* (May 1974) and brought gratifying responses from serious bass fisherman across the nation.

One thing I found especially sobering was the high mortality among bass. On average, only one in 6,000 survives to reach maturity. Death comes from many sources: relentless raids on nests by egg eaters; continuous attacks by a long list of predators, including wading and diving birds, snakes, otters, turtles, and carnivorous fishes (including other bass); dietary deficiencies; bacterial infections; birth malformations; water pollution;

carcinomas, melanomas, and tumors; black grubs, tapeworms, and attacks by countless protozoan parasites; and smothering by siltation. Add to this list the most efficient predator of all—man—and bass face a formidable struggle for survival.

Once we were proofing a film sequence with a powerful bass trying to guard a nest of eggs. Lau had followed this prime male though the phases of courtship, the nipping, nudging, and coaxing of a female onto a bed he had fanned until his tail was bloodied.

Romance followed, and when observed close-up, the spawning act was a fascinating ritual. Also observing close-up were many predacious fish, especially hordes of bluegills, waiting.

Once the eggs were spawned and fertilized, both bass protected them pugnaciously. They took turns guarding the nest and chasing away aggressive bluegills, until finally the female tired and deserted.

Alone, surrounded, harassed, and hopelessly outnumbered, the male bass fought to protect his brood until exhaustion overwhelmed him

A fatigued bass. Photograph by Glen Lau.

as well. Then he hovered close by, helpless, while a mob of bluegills moved in to suck up every egg.

Just another fish? Hardly. While I'm sure no one knows if a bass is capable of emotion, I could sense something of sorrow, even hopelessness, in this finned creature. His superb courage was not enough. And I mourned for him.

Then, in the closing scene, the camera closely followed a large female bass obviously having difficulty with equilibrium and locomotion. Spent by spawning, starved by a month of fasting while guarding the nest, infected by fungus and bacteria, she slowly settled to the bottom.

There, alone on a bed of eelgrass, the movements of fins and gills slowed. Finally, with a faint, final gasp, death came. I watched with moist eyes, grateful that the projection room was dark.

When the filming was finished and I returned to my bass-fishing haunts, I did so with a different feeling. Gone was the drive to complete that stringer mount. In its place was a far deeper understanding of, and an empathy for, my longtime adversary.

Now on those days when I fish all day without so much as a solid strike, I'm content, at peace inside, knowing that such days are necessary to the survival of all fish. And when I find bass in a feeding frenzy, I'm content to catch a couple and move away. I no longer kill a bass unless there's a reason.

Reasons like good friends, perhaps those ill or afflicted, who enjoy eating fresh fish. Or maybe a young fishing companion who catches a nice bass and wants to take it home to show mom. I remember as a lad how proud I was to furnish bass for a family supper.

Otherwise, I take every precaution to handle each bass I catch with consummate care and a concern for its survival. Knowing that my hand acid can remove the protective mucus from its body and induce fungal infection, I never touch a bass unless necessary.

Using a dehooking device or pair of long-nose pliers, I grasp the hook and shake off the bass whenever possible. When it must be handled, I do it with clean hands that have been neutralized with a salt solution.

Some will say, "None is purer than a reformed sinner. Why shouldn't you be magnanimous? Catching bass has been your vocation, and you have caught far more than your share."

There is some truth here. But perhaps if I can convey to others anglers, especially younger ones, an early respect and concern for each fish caught, the challenges, frustrations, and rewards of angling will come to have a different meaning. The more fishermen become concerned about the welfare of the fish they pursue, the more they will insist on a better environment for their survival.

Yes, today when I have outwitted or lucked into a bass, whether a trophy or a small one, I see more than just another fish. I see a blessing that has been mine for more than a half century. I see reasons for the countless times I have been wind-chilled, rain-soaked, sunburned, dog-tired, ridiculously late to supper, overspent on dollars needed elsewhere, neglectful of home chores, drowsy around guests, frustrated, and smelly.

I also see the essence of cherished friendships with men, women, and kids over four continents, all fifty states, and most of Canada. Places where in many cases we didn't speak the same language, yet we managed to communicate, compare methods, share knowledge, and establish close ties of lasting value because of the common bond all anglers share.

In addition, I cherish the formation of so many friendships with fishing buddies of unforgettable character. And most of them certainly were, and are, characters. Most of us can point to a host of friends, but a fishing buddy is something very special. Each of mine has in many ways made me a better person.

And now, as an elder angler, my ardor for fishing has not diminished. I'll pursue all sport species with the same vigor, the same insatiable quest for knowledge about each, in both near and faraway haunts. This has been my life and my blessing of a special livelihood.

As I catch varied species, I will handle each with a concern for its survival because I truly want it to live on. As I briefly hold and examine each, I see one of God's wondrous creatures—an animate being without words and for which I feel compelled to speak.

Just another fish? Not to these eyes, nor I hope to the eyes of my four grandchildren and others of their generation. An angling heritage awaits them, and the fish with all the mysteries that surround them will provide much-needed recreation for mind and body. May they enjoy them to the fullest and be concerned for these creatures that provide a lifetime of intrigue.

I will think of them as I look upon each fish I capture. Each is, in proportionate measure, theirs. As I watch it breathe and appear to return my gaze, I know we share one priceless gift: life.

And I feel moved to give it back the only thing I have to give, its life. That's the way it is now with me and a fish. Perhaps this feeling is simply a reverence for life. A giving instead of a taking. And I return home after each trip at peace in spirit and mind, a priceless gift from the One Great Fisherman and creator of all earthly creatures.

So let me bring this work to conclusion by sharing my favorite fisherman's prayer:

> God grant that I may fish
> until my dying day;
> and when at last I come to rest,
> I'll then most humbly pray;
> when in His landing net
> I lie in final sleep;
> that in His mercy I'll be judged
> as good enough to keep!
> Amen!

Index